MEDITERRANEAN DIET COOKBOOK FOR BEGINNERS

*Quick Recipes for Flavorful & Healthy Meals.
Surprise Yourself with a Healthy Cooking Journey*

SAMUEL HAYES

TABLE OF CONTENTS

INTRODUCTION 1

CHAPTER 1 : MEDITERRANEAN DIET 2

CHAPTER 2: BREAKFASTS AND SNACKS 7
- Pineapple, Banana, and Avocado Smoothie.. 9
- Avocado Toast.. 11
- Cherry, Beet, and Kale Smoothie... 13
- Greek Yogurt with Berries and Honey 15
- Vegetable and Feta Omelette... 17
- Horseradish Cheese and Tomato Toasts... 19
- Chocolate Peanut Butter Protein Smoothie 21
- Mediterranean Bruschetta 23
- Mediterranean Omelette.. 25
- Corn Polenta with Avocado 27
- Shakshuka.. 29
- Buckwheat Pudding with Mango Salsa 31
- Nutty Oatmeal with Fruits... 33
- Greek Yogurt with Strawberries and Chia Seeds 35
- Mushroom, Tomato, and Onion Frittata 37
- Spinach and Cheese Scrambled Eggs.. 39
- Seafood Omelette 41
- Zucchini Fritters with Feta and Olives 43
- Hot Mediterranean Sandwiches with Tomatoes and Mozzarella 45

CHAPTER 3: SALADS AND SOUPS 47
- Salad nicoise with Tuna and Egg 49
- Quinoa and Chickpea Salad with Baked Salmon....................................... 51
- Salad with Quail Eggs, Smoked Salmon, and Cherry Tomatoes 54
- Shrimp Salad with Melon, Watermelon, and Arugula 56
- Bean Salad... 58
- Tuna and Caper Salad 60
- Avocado and Crab Salad with Pine Nut Dressing 62
- Quinoa and Feta Vegetable Salad.. 64
- Warm Mediterranean Lamb Salad 66
- Chicken Spinach Soup.. 68
- Cheesy Shrimp and Herb Soup 70

Chickpea Soup with Calamari 72
Pumpkin Cream Soup with Shrimp 75
Mediterranean Tomato Soup with Squid 77
Light Spinach Soup Puree 80
Mussel Soup 82
Salmon in Curry Broth 84
Chilled Tomato Soup with Basil 86

CHAPTER 2 : MA`IN COURSES WITH FISH, MEAT, AND VEGETABLES 89

SIDE DISHES AND SAUCES 90

Cod with Tomatoes 91
Spaghetti with Shrimp and Pistachios 93
Pasta with Spinach and Salmon 95
Baked Beetroot with Brown Rice and Mozzarella 97
Turkey Breast with Egg and Cheese Sauce 99
Pan-seared salmon with Poached Egg, Brown Rice, and Vegetables 101
Grilled Lamb with Salad and Baked Potato with Egg 104
Carbonara Pizza 107
Falafel with Feta, Onion, Tomatoes, Hummus, and Rice 109
Chicken with Vegetables and Sweet Potato Fries 112
Pasta with Shrimp 115
Baked Duck Breast 117
Steamed Turkey with Rice 119
Vegetable Ragout with Baked Turkey 121
Baked Trout Recipe 124
Seabass with Potatoes, Capers, and Tomatoes 126
Rosemary Shrimp 128
Mediterranean Roasted Vegetable Lasagna 130
Cod with Celery Cream 133
Baked Dorado with Tomatoes and Capers 135
Dorado with Lemon 137
Tuna and Potato Casserole 139
Lamb with Beans and Green Beans 141
Mediterranean-style Mussels 143
Pan-fried calamari with Garlic and Olives 145
Beef Tenderloin with Rosemary 147
Pita Bread with Bean Hummus 149
Pan-Seared Halibut 151
Seabass with Leeks 153

Chicken with Mushrooms in Creamy Sauce 155
Grilled Tuna with Herb Aioli 157
Salmon and Avocado Tartare 159
Lamb with Plums 161
Grilled Shrimp Wrapped in Prosciutto 164
Sea Trout with Grilled Asparagus and Lemons 166

INTRODUCTION

Welcome to the world of the Mediterranean diet — a unique cultural and culinary tradition intricately tied to people's lives and health over centuries. This lifestyle embodies the diversity of flavors and aromas of Mediterranean cuisine and a philosophy of moderation and joy in every meal.

The Mediterranean diet is more than just a collection of recipes; it tells how people celebrate holidays, find joy in daily life, and care for their well-being through food. Rooted in abundant consumption of vegetables, fruits, olive oil, fish, nuts, and grains, this approach to eating is renowned for its positive impact on cardiovascular health and overall well-being.

In this book, you'll discover classic Mediterranean recipes, modern interpretations, and tips for achieving balance and harmony in every dish. We explore a wide range of recipes inspired by Mediterranean cuisine, each designed to capture the essence of this vibrant and healthful way of eating. Whether you want to expand your culinary repertoire or embark on a journey to improve your health, the Mediterranean diet offers a delicious and sustainable path to achieving your goals. Welcome to the world of Mediterranean cuisine, where every meal celebrates taste, nourishment, and well-being. Get ready to immerse yourself in a world of flavor, health, and culinary pleasure that embodies the Mediterranean lifestyle.

CHAPTER 1 : MEDITERRANEAN DIET

What is the Mediterranean diet?

The Mediterranean diet is a style of eating based on the traditional culinary habits and lifestyle of countries in the Mediterranean region, such as Greece, Italy, Spain, and Southern France. This eating strategy has become more well-known because of its many health advantages and correlation with long life.

Among the fundamental tenets of the Mediterranean diet are:

- **A diet rich in vegetables and fruits:** Fruits and vegetables are the foundation of every diet since they supply the body with vital nutrients, including vitamins, minerals, and antioxidants.
- Olive oil is the principal fat source and supports cardiovascular health since it is high in antioxidants and monounsaturated fats.
- _Seafood and fish:_ Fish and seafood are the primary sources of protein and omega-3 fatty acids, which are proven to lower inflammation and support heart health.
- _Nuts and seeds:_ Rich in healthy fats, proteins, and fiber, nuts and seeds are an essential part of the diet.
- _Whole grains:_ The significant sources of fiber and carbs are whole-grain products, including bread, pasta, rice, and other grains.
- _Moderate consumption of dairy products:_ Cheese and other dairy products should be taken in moderation.
- _Poultry and eggs:_ Poultry and eggs are also part of the diet, but their consumption is usually moderate compared to fish and seafood.
- _Red meat and sweets:_ Consumption of red meat and sweets is limited, being eaten rarely and in small quantities.
- _Wine:_ Moderate consumption of red wine, typically during meals, is a common practice in Mediterranean countries.
- _Physical activity and social aspects:_ The Mediterranean diet also includes an active lifestyle and an emphasis on enjoying meals with family and friends.

One of the world's healthiest diets is the Mediterranean diet. Research has shown that it helps reduce the risk of cardiovascular diseases, diabetes, and cancer and promotes maintaining a healthy weight and improving cognitive functions.

Health Benefits of the Mediterranean Diet:

- Enhancement of cognitive functions
- Prevention of type 2 diabetes
- Combating metabolic syndrome
- Prevention of cardiovascular diseases
- Promoting a long and quality life

1. Strengthens the Heart

Spanish researchers invited 7,447 volunteers aged 55-80 at increased risk of developing cardiovascular diseases for their study. Three distinct diets were presented to the participants: a low-fat diet, a Mediterranean diet emphasizing nuts, and a Mediterranean diet enhanced with extra virgin olive oil. Over the next five years, the specialists monitored the participants' health.

The results showed that those who followed the Mediterranean diet had nearly a one-third reduction in the risk of stroke and heart attack. According to the researchers, the diet helps remove "bad" cholesterol from the body and normalizes blood pressure and blood sugar levels.

2. Helps in Preventing Diabetes

The same researchers attempted to determine how the Mediterranean diet affects the onset of type 2 diabetes. They assessed the health of 418 people who did not have the disease at the start of the study. Among those who chose the Mediterranean diet, the likelihood of developing type 2 diabetes was 52% lower compared to those who followed a low-fat diet.

3. Improves Gut Health

According to a study by an international group of scientists, the Mediterranean diet positively affects gut microbiota. The specialists monitored the health of 612 people aged 65-79 from Poland, the UK, the Netherlands, France, and Italy. The subjects followed the Mediterranean diet for a year. As a result, they experienced a slower loss of bacterial diversity, increased "good" bacteria and beneficial fatty acids, and decreased chemical compounds that cause inflammation and bacteria in forming bile acids.

4. Extends Life

Cardiologists from the University Hospital in Saint-Etienne (France) discovered that eating a Mediterranean diet decreases the chance of dying young.

The study involved 605 people who had suffered a heart attack six months prior. They were offered two dietary options: a low-fat diet and the Mediterranean diet. The researchers monitored the patients' health for four years. In the Mediterranean diet group, mortality risk from all causes was reduced by 45% and heart disease by 70%.

5. Helps with Weight Loss

The Mediterranean diet allows for weight normalization without calorie counting. Scientists from the Second University of Naples reached this conclusion. The study involved 99 men and 81 women, divided into two groups. One group was required to adhere to the recommended intake of proteins, carbohydrates, and fats. In contrast, the other group was instructed to increase their consumption of whole grain products, nuts, fruits, vegetables, and olive oil. After two years, the researchers evaluated the results: weight loss in the Mediterranean diet group was three times greater.

CHAPTER 2: BREAKFASTS AND SNACKS

PINEAPPLE, BANANA, AND AVOCADO SMOOTHIE

Ingredients:

- 1 ripe banana
- 1 ripe avocado
- 1 cup pineapple chunks (fresh or frozen)
- Need to add 1 cup of coconut milk (or any other plant-based milk)
- 1/2 cup Greek yogurt (optional for creaminess)
- One tablespoon of maple honey or syrup, if desired, for sweetness
- Ice (optional for cooling)

Directions:

1. Peel the banana and avocado, remove the pit from the avocado, and cut them into pieces.
2. Combine the banana, avocado, pineapple chunks, coconut milk, and yogurt in a blender.
3. Incorporate honey or maple syrup to achieve a higher level of sweetness.
4. Process quickly until smooth and creamy. If desired, add ice and blend again until fully incorporated.
5. Immediately serve the smoothie by pouring it into glasses

Prep Time:

- Preparation: 5 minutes
- Total: 5 minutes

Servings:

- Number of servings: 2

Nutrition Information (per serving):

- Calories: approximately 250-300 kcal
- Protein: 5-6 g
- Fat: 10-12 g
- Carbohydrates: 30-35 g
- Fiber: 5-6 g
- Sugar: 15-20 g

AVOCADO TOAST

Ingredients:

- 1 ripe avocado
- 2 slices of whole-grain or sourdough bread
- 1 tablespoon olive oil (optional)
- Salt and pepper to taste

Optional toppings:

- Cherry tomatoes, halved
- Crumbled feta or goat cheese
- Red pepper flakes
- Poached or fried egg
- Fresh herbs (e.g., cilantro, parsley)
- Lemon juice

Directions:

1. Toast the slices of bread to your desired level of crispiness.
2. While the bread is browing, cut the avocado in half, remove the pit, and ladle the meat into a bowl.
3. Using a fork, mash the avocado until it has the consistency you want (chunky or smooth).
4. If using, drizzle the mashed avocado with olive oil and mix well.
5. Season the avocado mash with salt and pepper to taste.
6. Evenly top the toast with a layer of mashed avocado.
7. Add any optional toppings you like.

8. Serve immediately.

Prep Time:
- Preparation: 5 minutes
- Total: 5 minutes

Servings:
- Number of servings: 2

Nutrition Information (per serving):
- Calories: approximately 250-300 kcal
- Protein: 4-6 g
- Fat: 15-20 g
- Carbohydrates: 20-25 g
- Fiber: 7-9 g
- Sugar: 2-3 g

CHERRY, BEET, AND KALE SMOOTHIE

Ingredients:

- 1 cup fresh or frozen cherries, pitted
- 1 small beet, peeled and chopped
- 1 cup kale leaves, stems removed
- 1 banana
- One cup of unsweetened almond milk
- 1 tablespoon chia seeds (optional for added nutrition)
- One tablespoon of honey (maple syrup)
- Ice (optional for cooling)

Directions:

1. Prepare the ingredients by pitting the cherries, peeling and chopping the beet, and removing the stems from the kale leaves.
2. Place the cherries, chopped beet, kale leaves, banana, and almond milk in a blender.
3. Incorporate the chia seeds and, if desired, honey or maple syrup.
4. Process on high speed until creamy and smooth.
5. Add some ice to your smoothie and mix until it's completely blended if you want it cooler.
6. Pour the smoothie into glasses.

Prep Time:

- Preparation: 10 minutes
- Total: 10 minutes

Servings:
- Number of servings: 2

Nutrition Information (per serving):
- Calories: approximately 150-200 kcal
- Protein: 3-5 g
- Fat: 2-3 g
- Carbohydrates: 30-35 g
- Fiber: 6-8 g
- Sugar: 15-20 g

GREEK YOGURT WITH BERRIES AND HONEY

Ingredients:

- 1 cup Greek yogurt
- Half a cup of mixed fresh berries, including blackberries, raspberries, blueberries, or strawberries
- 1-2 tablespoons honey
- 1/4 cup granola (optional for crunch)
- 1 tablespoon chopped nuts (optional for extra texture and protein)
- Fresh mint leaves (optional for garnish)

Directions:

1. Spoon the Greek yogurt into a serving bowl.
2. After rinsing, carefully pat the fresh berries dry.
3. Arrange the berries on top of the yogurt.
4. Drizzle honey over the berries and yogurt.
5. For texture and crunch, sprinkle chopped nuts and granola over top.
6. Garnish with fresh mint leaves if using.
7. Serve immediately.

Prep Time:

- Preparation: 5 minutes
- Total: 5 minutes

Servings:

- Number of servings: 1

Nutrition Information (per serving):

- Calories: approximately 200-250 kcal
- Protein: 10-12 g
- Fat: 5-7 g
- Carbohydrates: 30-35 g
- Fiber: 3-5 g
- Sugar: 20-25 g

VEGETABLE AND FETA OMELETTE

Ingredients:

- 3 large eggs
- 1/4 cup milk (optional for fluffiness)
- Half a cup of finely chopped red, green, or yellow bell peppers
- 1/2 cup diced tomatoes
- 1/4 cup chopped spinach or kale
- 1/4 cup crumbled feta cheese
- 1 tablespoon olive oil or butter
- Salt and pepper to taste
- Fresh herbs (optional for garnish, such as parsley or chives)

Directions:

1. Mix the eggs with a whisk of milk (if using), salt, and pepper until thoroughly blended.
2. In a nonstick skillet, preheat the butter or olive oil over medium heat.
3. Cook the chopped bell peppers for two to three minutes or until they soften.
4. Add the chopped spinach or kale and diced tomatoes to the pan once the greens have wilted, then simmer for an additional minute or two.
5. Cover the veggies in the pan with the egg mixture. Cook, uncovered, for one to two minutes or until the edges begin to set.
6. Evenly distribute the feta cheese crumbles on top of the omelet.

7. Lift the omelet's edges slightly with a spatula to let the raw eggs slide below. Continue cooking for 2-3 minutes until the eggs are fully set.
8. After folding the omelet in half, transfer it to a dish.
9. Garnish with fresh herbs.

Prep Time:

- Preparation: 10 minutes
- Cooking: 5-7 minutes
- Total: 15-17 minutes

Servings:

- Number of servings: 1

Nutrition Information (per serving):

- Calories: approximately 300-350 kcal
- Protein: 18-20 g
- Fat: 20-25 g
- Carbohydrates: 8-10 g
- Fiber: 2-3 g
- Sugar: 4-5 g

HORSERADISH CHEESE AND TOMATO TOASTS

Ingredients:

- 4 slices of whole-grain or sourdough bread
- 1 cup grated horseradish cheese (or any sharp cheese mixed with a bit of prepared horseradish)
- 2 medium tomatoes, thinly sliced
- 1 tablespoon olive oil
- Salt and pepper to taste
- Fresh basil leaves (optional for garnish)

Directions:

1. Set the oven temperature to 375°F, or 190°C.
2. Place the bread slices on a baking sheet and brush each slice lightly with olive oil.
3. Bake the bread for five minutes or until it's crispy and brown.
4. Take the baking sheet from the oven and put the grated horseradish cheese on each slice of bread. Spread it evenly.
5. Arrange the tomato slices on the cheese, overlapping slightly if necessary.
6. Sprinkle a little salt and pepper on the tomato slices.
7. Put the baking sheet back in the oven and continue to bake for five to seven minutes or until the cheese is bubbling and melted.
8. Take the toasts out of the oven and give them a little time to cool.
9. If using, garnish with fresh basil leaves and serve right away.

Prep Time:
- Preparation: 5 minutes
- Cooking: 10-12 minutes
- Total: 15-17 minutes

Servings:
- Number of servings: 2

Nutrition Information (per serving):
- Calories: approximately 200-250 kcal
- Protein: 10-12 g
- Fat: 10-12 g
- Carbohydrates: 20-25 g
- Fiber: 3-4 g
- Sugar: 3-4 g

CHOCOLATE PEANUT BUTTER PROTEIN SMOOTHIE

Ingredients:
- One cup of unsweetened plant-based milk, such as almond milk.
- 1 ripe banana
- 2 tablespoons natural peanut butter
- 1 scoop of chocolate protein powder
- 1 tablespoon unsweetened cocoa powder
- 1 tablespoon chia seeds (optional for added nutrition)
- 1/2 teaspoon vanilla extract
- Ice (optional for cooling)
- Your preferred sweetener, such as stevia or honey (optional)

Directions:
1. Add the almond milk, banana, peanut butter, protein powder, cocoa powder, chia seeds (if using), and vanilla extract to a blender.
2. Process on high speed until creamy and smooth.
3. Add some ice to the smoothie and mix until it's completely blended if you want it cooler.
4. After tasting the smoothie, add the appropriate sweetener and blend one more to ensure a smooth consistency.
5. Transfer the smoothie into cups and start serving right away.

Prep Time:
- Preparation: 5 minutes
- Total: 5 minutes

Servings:
- Number of servings: 1

Nutrition Information (per serving):
- Calories: approximately 350-400 kcal
- Protein: 25-30 g
- Fat: 12-15 g
- Carbohydrates: 30-35 g
- Fiber: 7-9 g
- Sugar: 15-20 g

MEDITERRANEAN BRUSCHETTA

Ingredients:

- 1 baguette or ciabatta loaf, sliced into 1/2-inch thick pieces
- 1 cup cherry tomatoes, halved
- 1/2 cup diced cucumber
- 1/4 cup diced red onion
- One-quarter cup chopped and pitted Kalamata olives
- 1/4 cup crumbled feta cheese
- 2 tablespoons extra virgin olive oil
- 1 tablespoon balsamic vinegar
- 1 clove garlic, minced
- Fresh basil leaves, chopped (optional)
- Salt and pepper to taste

Directions:

1. Turn the oven on to 375°F (190°C).
2. Arrange the baguette slices on a baking pan and brush with a small amount of olive oil.
3. Bake the bread for five to seven minutes or until it's crispy and brown.
4. While the bread is toasting, prepare the topping. Combine the cherry tomatoes, cucumber, red onion, Kalamata olives, feta cheese, olive oil, balsamic vinegar, and minced garlic in a medium bowl.
5. Combine by tossing, then season to taste with salt and pepper.
6. Take out the toasted bread and give it a little time to cool.

7. Spoon the Mediterranean mixture onto each slice of toasted bread.
8. Garnish with fresh basil leaves if desired.
9. Serve immediately.

Prep Time:

- Preparation: 10 minutes
- Cooking: 5-7 minutes
- Total: 15-17 minutes

Servings:

- Number of servings: 4-6 (depending on the size of the bread slices)

Nutrition Information (per serving):

- Calories: approximately 150-200 kcal
- Protein: 4-6 g
- Fat: 8-10 g
- Carbohydrates: 15-20 g
- Fiber: 2-3 g
- Sugar: 2-3 g

MEDITERRANEAN OMELETTE

Ingredients:

- 3 large eggs
- 1/4 cup milk (optional for fluffiness)
- 1/4 cup chopped red, yellow, or green bell peppers
- 1/4 cup diced tomatoes
- 1/4 cup chopped spinach or kale
- 1/4 cup crumbled feta cheese
- 1/4 cup sliced Kalamata olives
- 1 tablespoon olive oil or butter
- Salt and pepper to taste
- Fresh basil or parsley (optional for garnish)

Directions:

1. Completely combine the eggs, milk (if using), salt, and pepper in a medium-sized bowl.
2. In a nonstick skillet, preheat the butter or olive oil over medium heat.
3. Cook the chopped bell peppers in the pan for two to three minutes or until they become tender.
4. Cook the chopped spinach or kale for a further minute or two, or until the greens are wilted, after adding the diced tomatoes to the pan.
5. Pour the egg mixture over the vegetables in the skillet. Let it cook undisturbed for about 1-2 minutes until the edges start to set.
6. Sprinkle the crumbled feta cheese and sliced Kalamata olives evenly over the top of the omelet.

7. Lift the omelet's edges with a spatula to let the raw eggs slide below. Continue cooking for 2-3 minutes until the eggs are fully set.
8. Slide the omelet onto a plate after folding it in half.
9. If wanted, garnish with fresh parsley or basil and serve right away.

Prep Time:
- Preparation: 10 minutes
- Cooking: 5-7 minutes
- Total: 15-17 minutes

Servings:
- Number of servings: 1

Nutrition Information (per serving):
- Calories: approximately 300-350 kcal
- Protein: 18-20 g
- Fat: 20-25 g
- Carbohydrates: 8-10 g
- Fiber: 2-3 g
- Sugar: 4-5 g

CORN POLENTA WITH AVOCADO

Ingredients:

- 1 cup cornmeal
- 4 cups water or vegetable broth
- 1 ripe avocado
- 1 tablespoon olive oil
- Salt and pepper to taste

Optional toppings:

- Cherry tomatoes, halved
- Fresh herbs (e.g., cilantro, parsley)
- Red pepper flakes
- Grated Parmesan cheese

Directions:

1. In a medium saucepan, bring the water or vegetable broth to a boil.
2. Add the cornmeal gradually while whisking continuously to avoid lumps.
3. Minimize the heat to a simmer and cook the polenta, stirring often, until it thickens and takes on a creamy texture, 15 to 20 minutes.
4. While the polenta is cooking, prepare the avocado. Scoop the avocado's flesh into a bowl after cutting it open and removing the pit. Use a fork to mash the avocado until it's smooth.
5. Take the polenta from the heat and whisk in the olive oil once it reaches the correct consistency. Season with salt and pepper to taste.
6. Serve the polenta hot, topped with mashed avocado and any optional toppings.

7. If wanted, garnish with a drizzle of olive oil and fresh herbs.
8. Serve immediately.

Prep Time:
- Preparation: 5 minutes
- Cooking: 15-20 minutes
- Total: 20-25 minutes

Servings:
- Number of servings: 4

Nutrition Information (per serving, without optional toppings):
- Calories: approximately 200 kcal
- Protein: 4 g
- Fat: 7 g
- Carbohydrates: 31 g
- Fiber: 4 g
- Sugar: 1 g

SHAKSHUKA

Ingredients:

- 1 tablespoon olive oil
- 1 onion, finely chopped
- 1 red bell pepper, diced
- 3 cloves garlic, minced
- 1 teaspoon ground cumin
- 1 teaspoon paprika
- Half a teaspoon, or according to taste, chili powder
- 1 can (14 oz) crushed tomatoes
- 4-6 eggs
- Salt and pepper to taste
- Fresh parsley or cilantro, chopped (for garnish)
- Crumbled feta cheese (optional for garnish)
- Crusty bread or pita for serving

Directions:

1. Heat the olive oil in a large skillet or frying pan over medium heat.
2. Add diced red bell pepper and minced onion. Cook until softened, stirring often, for 5 to 7 minutes.
3. Add minced garlic, ground cumin, paprika, and chili powder. Cook for 1-2 minutes until fragrant.
4. Pour in the crushed tomatoes and stir well—season with salt and pepper to taste.
5. Simmer the tomato mixture for ten to fifteen minutes, or until it begins to thicken slightly, over medium heat.

6. Using a spoon, create small wells in the tomato mixture and carefully crack one egg into each well. Give each egg a little pinch of salt and pepper.
7. Place a cover on the skillet and cook the eggs for 5 to 8 minutes over medium-low heat or until the yolks are still runny but the whites are set (cook longer if you want hard yolks).
8. Remove the skillet from heat. Sprinkle chopped parsley or cilantro over the top.
9. If desired, garnish with crumbled feta cheese.
10. Present warm, along with crusty bread or pita chips for dipping.

Prep Time:

- Preparation: 10 minutes
- Cooking: 25 minutes
- Total: 35 minutes

Servings:

- Number of servings: 4

Nutrition Information (per serving, without bread or cheese):

- Calories: approximately 180 kcal
- Protein: 9 g
- Fat: 10 g
- Carbohydrates: 14 g
- Fiber: 4 g
- Sugar: 8 g

BUCKWHEAT PUDDING WITH MANGO SALSA

Ingredients:

- 1 cup buckwheat groats
- 2 cups water
- 1/4 teaspoon salt
- 1 ripe mango, peeled and diced
- 1/2 red bell pepper, finely chopped
- 1/4 cup red onion, finely chopped
- 1/4 cup fresh cilantro, chopped
- Juice of 1 lime
- Salt and pepper to taste

Directions:

1. Rinse the buckwheat groats under cold water.
2. Place two cups of water in a medium pot and heat to a boil. Add the salt and washed buckwheat groats.
3. Minimize the heat to low, cover, and simmer for 15-20 minutes or until the buckwheat is tender and the water is absorbed. Take it off the heat and leave it covered for five minutes.
4. Fluff the cooked buckwheat with a fork and let it cool slightly.
5. In a mixing dish, combine the diced mango, chopped red onion, red bell pepper, cilantro, lime juice, salt, and pepper.
6. Mix well to combine.
7. Topped with mango salsa, serve the cooked buckwheat groats warm or at room temperature.

Prep Time:
- Preparation: 10 minutes
- Cooking: 20 minutes
- Total: 30 minutes

Servings:
- Number of servings: 4

Nutrition Information (per serving):
- Calories: approximately 180 kcal
- Protein: 5 g
- Fat: 1 g
- Carbohydrates: 40 g
- Fiber: 6 g
- Sugar: 9 g

NUTTY OATMEAL WITH FRUITS

Ingredients:

- 1 cup old-fashioned rolled oats
- Two glasses of water or plant-based or dairy milk
- 1/4 cup chopped nuts (walnuts, almonds, or pecans)
- 1/4 cup dried fruits (raisins, cranberries, or chopped apricots)
- One tablespoon of maple syrup or honey, if desired, for sweetness
- 1/2 teaspoon ground cinnamon (optional)
- Fresh fruits for topping (sliced bananas, berries, or diced apples)

Directions:

1. In a medium saucepan, bring the water or milk to a boil.
2. Turn the heat down to medium-low and stir in the rolled oats.
3. Cook the oats for five to seven minutes, stirring now and again, or until they are soft and creamy.
4. In a dry pan over medium heat, toast the chopped nuts for two to three minutes or until fragrant and browned. This will happen while the oats cook. Set aside.
5. After the oats are cooked, take the skillet off of the stove and mix in the chopped nuts, dried fruits, ground cinnamon, honey, or maple syrup, if using.
6. Divide the oatmeal into serving bowls.
7. Top each bowl with fresh fruits of your choice.
8. Serve warm and enjoy!

Prep Time:
- Preparation: 5 minutes
- Cooking: 10 minutes
- Total: 15 minutes

Servings:
- Number of servings: 2

Nutrition Information (per serving):
- Calories: approximately 300 kcal
- Protein: 8 g
- Fat: 10 g
- Carbohydrates: 50 g
- Fiber: 7 g
- Sugar: 15 g

GREEK YOGURT WITH STRAWBERRIES AND CHIA SEEDS

Ingredients:
- 1 cup Greek yogurt
- 1/2 cup fresh strawberries, sliced
- 1 tablespoon chia seeds
- For sweetness - One tablespoon of maple syrup or honey,
- Fresh mint leaves (optional, for garnish)

Directions:
1. Spoon the Greek yogurt onto a bowl or serving plate.
2. Arrange the sliced strawberries on top of the yogurt.
3. Sprinkle chia seeds evenly over the strawberries.
4. If desired, drizzle honey or maple syrup over the top for added sweetness.
5. Garnish with fresh mint leaves if using.
6. Serve immediately and enjoy!

Prep Time:
- Preparation: 5 minutes
- Total: 5 minutes

Servings:
- Number of servings: 1

Nutrition Information (per serving):

- Calories: approximately 200 kcal
- Protein: 15 g
- Fat: 6 g
- Carbohydrates: 25 g
- Fiber: 5 g
- Sugar: 15 g

MUSHROOM, TOMATO, AND ONION FRITTATA

Ingredients:

- 6 large eggs
- 1/2 cup milk or cream
- 1 cup sliced mushrooms (any variety)
- 1 cup cherry tomatoes, halved
- 1/2 cup diced onion
- 1 tablespoon olive oil or butter
- Salt and pepper to taste
- 1/4 cup grated Parmesan cheese (optional)
- Fresh herbs, chopped (for garnish, such as thyme or parsley).

Directions:

1. Preheat your oven to 350°F (175°C).
2. In a large bowl, thoroughly mix the eggs, milk or cream, salt, and pepper. Put aside.
3. In a medium oven-safe skillet, preheat the butter or olive oil over medium heat. Fill the skillet with the chopped onion and sliced mushrooms. Simmer until the onions are translucent and the mushrooms are tender, stirring often, for 5 to 7 minutes.
4. After adding the cherry tomatoes, cook them for two to three minutes in the pan.
5. Evenly distribute the egg mixture over the skillet's veggies. To uniformly spread the ingredients, whisk gently.
6. Simmer the frittata for three to four minutes or until the edges begin to firm.
7. Sprinkle grated Parmesan cheese evenly over the top if using.
8. Place the pan in the oven that has been prepared, and bake for 15 to 20 minutes, or until the frittata is set in the middle and has a gently browned top.
9. Remove from the oven and let it cool slightly before slicing.

10. Garnish with fresh chopped herbs, if desired.
11. Serve warm or at room temperature.

Prep Time:

- Preparation: 10 minutes
- Cooking: 25-30 minutes
- Total: 35-40 minutes

Servings:

- Number of servings: 4-6

Nutrition Information (per serving, based on 4 servings):

- Calories: approximately 180 kcal
- Protein: 12 g
- Fat: 11 g
- Carbohydrates: 8 g
- Fiber: 2 g
- Sugar: 4 g

SPINACH AND CHEESE SCRAMBLED EGGS

Ingredients:

- 4 eggs
- 1 cup fresh spinach leaves, chopped
- 1/4 cup shredded cheese (cheddar, mozzarella, or feta)
- 1 tablespoon butter or olive oil
- Salt and pepper to taste
- Fresh herbs (optional for garnish)

Directions:

1. Break the eggs open and gently beat with a fork or whisk in a bowl; season with salt and pepper.
2. In a nonstick skillet, preheat the butter or olive oil over medium heat.
3. Add the chopped spinach to the skillet and heat it for one to two minutes or until it wilts.
4. Pour the beaten eggs over the spinach in the skillet.
5. Until the eggs begin to set around the edges, let them simmer for a few seconds without stirring.
6. Using a spatula, gently mix the eggs, moving them from the skillet's rims into its middle. Continue occasionally cooking and stirring until the eggs are mostly set but slightly runny.
7. Evenly distribute the cheese shreds over the eggs.
8. Continue cooking for another 1-2 minutes or until the cheese is melted and the eggs are cooked to your desired consistency.
9. Turn off the heat source and slide the scrambled eggs onto a platter.
10. Garnish with fresh herbs if using.

11. Serve immediately.

Prep Time:
- Preparation: 5 minutes
- Cooking: 5 minutes
- Total: 10 minutes

Servings:
- Number of servings: 2

Nutrition Information (per serving):
- Calories: approximately 200 kcal
- Protein: 14 g
- Fat: 15 g
- Carbohydrates: 2 g
- Fiber: 1 g
- Sugar: 1

SEAFOOD OMELETTE

Ingredients:

- 3 large eggs
- 1/4 cup milk or cream
- 1/2 cup mixed seafood (such as shrimp, crab meat, or scallops), cooked and chopped
- 1/4 cup of chopped red, green, or yellow bell peppers
- 1/4 cup diced tomatoes
- 1/4 cup of shredded cheese, such as mozzarella or cheddar1 tablespoon butter or olive oil
- Salt and pepper to taste
- Fresh herbs (optional for garnish)

Directions:

1. In a medium-sized bowl, thoroughly combine the eggs, milk or cream, salt, and pepper.
2. In a nonstick skillet, preheat the butter or olive oil over medium heat.
3. Diced bell peppers need to be added to the skillet and sauté for 2-3 minutes until they soften.
4. Add diced tomatoes and mixed seafood to the skillet. Cook for another 2-3 minutes until heated through.
5. Pour the egg mixture evenly over the seafood and vegetables in the skillet.
6. Cook, uncovered, for one to two minutes or until the edges begin to firm.
7. Use a spatula to gently raise the omelet's borders so that the raw eggs may slide below.
8. Sprinkle shredded cheese evenly over the omelet.

9. Cook for a further two to three minutes or until the cheese has melted and the eggs are set.
10. After folding the omelet in half, transfer it to a dish.
11. Garnish with fresh herbs if using.
12. Serve immediately.

Prep Time:

- Preparation: 10 minutes
- Cooking: 10 minutes
- Total: 20 minutes

Servings:

- Number of servings: 1

Nutrition Information (per serving):

- Calories: approximately 350 kcal
- Protein: 30 g
- Fat: 22 g
- Carbohydrates: 8 g
- Fiber: 2 g
- Sugar: 4 g

ZUCCHINI FRITTERS WITH FETA AND OLIVES

Ingredients:

- 2 medium zucchinis, grated
- 1/2 cup crumbled feta cheese
- 1/4 cup chopped Kalamata olives
- 1/4 cup chopped fresh parsley
- 2 cloves garlic, minced
- 2 eggs
- 1/4 cup all-purpose flour or breadcrumbs
- Salt and pepper to taste
- Olive oil for frying

Directions:

1. Prepare the Zucchini Mixture:

- Transfer the finely chopped zucchini to a sieve and season with salt. Let them sit for about 10 minutes to release excess moisture. Squeeze out as much juice as you can from the zucchini.
- In a big bowl, mix together the shredded zucchini, crumbled feta cheese, chopped parsley, olives, minced garlic, eggs, flour or breadcrumbs, salt, and pepper. Mix well until everything is evenly combined.

2. Cook the Fritters:

- In a big, nonstick skillet, heat a thin coating of olive oil over medium heat.

- Using a spatula, gently flatten approximately 1/4 cup of the zucchini mixture into a spherical shape before adding it to the skillet. Repeat to make more cakes, leaving some space between each in the skillet.
- Cook for 3-4 minutes on each side or until the cakes are crispy and golden brown. These can require batch cooking, depending on the size of your skillet.
- To absorb extra oil, move the cooked patties to a dish covered with paper towels.

3. Serve:

- Serve the heated zucchini fritters with more chopped parsley or crumbled feta cheese on top, if preferred.
- They can be enjoyed plain or with yogurt sauce or tzatziki.

Prep Time:

- Preparation: 15 minutes
- Cooking: 15 minutes
- Total: 30 minutes

Servings:

- Number of servings: Makes about 10 fritters

Nutrition Information (per serving, 2 cakes):

- Calories: approximately 180 kcal
- Protein: 8 g
- Fat: 10 g
- Carbohydrates: 15 g
- Fiber: 2 g
- Sugar: 3 g

HOT MEDITERRANEAN SANDWICHES WITH TOMATOES AND MOZZARELLA

Ingredients:

- 4 ciabatta rolls or other sandwich rolls
- 2 large tomatoes, thinly sliced
- 8 oz (225g) fresh mozzarella cheese, sliced
- 2 tablespoons basil pesto
- 2 tablespoons olive oil
- Salt and pepper to taste
- Fresh basil leaves, for garnish (optional)

Directions:

1. Prepare the Sandwiches:

- Turn the oven on to 375°F, or 190°C.
- Slice the ciabatta rolls horizontally and lay them open on a baking sheet.

2. Assemble the Sandwiches:

- Spread a thin basil pesto layer on each roll's bottom half.
- Layer tomato slices and mozzarella slices evenly over the pesto.

3. Season and Bake:

- Drizzle the mozzarella and tomato layers with olive oil.
- Season with salt and pepper to taste.

4. Bake the Sandwiches:
- Put the constructed sandwiches in the oven that has been preheated.
- Bake for 10 to 12 minutes or until the bread is gently toasted and the cheese is melted and bubbling.

5. Serve:
- Take it out of the oven and allow it to cool a little.
- Optionally, garnish with fresh basil leaves.
- Serve hot and enjoy!

Prep Time:
- Preparation: 10 minutes
- Cooking: 10-12 minutes
- Total: 20-22 minutes

Servings:
- Number of servings: 4 sandwiches

Nutrition Information (per serving):
- Calories: approximately 400 kcal
- Protein: 18 g
- Fat: 20 g
- Carbohydrates: 35 g
- Fiber: 2 g
- Sugar: 3 g

CHAPTER 3: SALADS AND SOUPS

SALAD NICOISE WITH TUNA AND EGG

Ingredients:

- 8 oz (225g) fresh tuna steak
- Four cups of mixed salad greens, including spinach, arugula, and lettuce
- 1 cup cherry tomatoes, halved
- 1/2 cup green beans, blanched and halved
- 1/4 cup black olives (preferably Niçoise olives)
- 2 hard-boiled eggs, peeled and quartered
- 2 tablespoons capers
- Two tablespoons of freshly chopped parsley, if desired, as a garnish
- Lemon wedges (for serving)

For the Dressing:

- 1/4 cup extra virgin olive oil
- Two teaspoons of lemon juice or red wine vinegar
- 1 teaspoon Dijon mustard
- 1 clove garlic, minced
- Salt and pepper to taste

Directions:

1. Prepare the Tuna:

- Season the tuna steak on both sides with salt and pepper.
- Heat a grill pan or skillet over medium-high heat.

- Cook the tuna steak for 2-3 minutes per side or until desired doneness (medium-rare is recommended). Remove from heat and let it rest for a few minutes before slicing.

2. Prepare the Salad:

- Arrange the mixed salad greens as the base in a large salad bowl.
- Arrange cherry tomatoes, blanched green beans, black olives, and quartered hard-boiled eggs around the greens.

3. Assemble the Salad:

- Slice the grilled tuna steak into thin slices and place them on the salad.
- Sprinkle capers evenly over the salad.

4. Prepare the Dressing:

- In a small bowl, mix together olive oil, Dijon mustard, lemon juice, or red wine vinegar, chopped garlic, salt, and pepper.

5. Serve:

- Just before serving, pour the dressing over the salad.
- Garnish with chopped fresh parsley, if using.
- Serve it with lemon wedges on the side.

Prep Time:

- Preparation: 15 minutes
- Cooking (for tuna): 6 minutes (including resting time)
- Total: 20-25 minutes

Servings:

- Number of servings: 2

Nutrition Information (per serving):

- Calories: approximately 450 kcal
- Protein: 35 g
- Fat: 30 g
- Carbohydrates: 12 g
- Fiber: 4 g
- Sugar: 4 g

QUINOA AND CHICKPEA SALAD WITH BAKED SALMON

Ingredients:

- 1 cup quinoa, rinsed
- 2 cups water or vegetable broth
- 1 lb salmon fillet, skinless
- 1 tablespoon olive oil
- Salt and pepper to taste
- 1 can (15 oz) chickpeas, drained and rinsed
- 1 cucumber, diced
- 1 bell pepper (any color), diced
- 1/4 cup red onion, finely chopped
- 1/4 cup fresh parsley, chopped
- 1/4 cup feta cheese, crumbled (optional)
- Lemon wedges (for serving)

For the Dressing:

- 1/4 cup extra virgin olive oil
- 2 tablespoons lemon juice
- 1 tablespoon Dijon mustard
- 1 clove garlic, minced
- Salt and pepper to taste

Directions:

1. Prepare the Quinoa:

- Boil two cups of water or vegetable broth in a medium pot.
- After washing the quinoa, add it and simmer it for 15 to 20 minutes, or until the liquid is absorbed while reducing the heat to low and covering. Use a fork, fluff, and allow it to cool somewhat.

2. Prepare the Salmon:

- Set the oven temperature to 200°C or 400°F.
- Arrange the salmon fillet on a parchment paper-lined baking sheet.
- Drizzle the salmon with olive oil after seasoning it with salt and pepper.
- Bake the salmon for 12 to 15 minutes, or until it is cooked through, and flake readily with a fork. Take it out of the oven and allow it to cool a little before breaking it into pieces.

3. Assemble the Salad:

- In a large salad bowl, mix cooked quinoa, chickpeas, sliced cucumber, bell pepper, chopped red onion, and chopped parsley.
- Add the flaked salmon chunks to the salad bowl.

4. Prepare the Dressing:

- In a small bowl, whisk together extra virgin olive oil, lemon juice, Dijon mustard, minced garlic, salt, and pepper.

5. Serve:

- Drizzle the dressing over the salad and toss gently to coat.
- Sprinkle crumbled feta cheese over the salad, if using.
- Present lemon wedges on the side so that guests can squeeze them over the salad.

Prep Time:

- Preparation: 15 minutes
- Cooking (for quinoa and salmon): 30 minutes
- Total: 45 minutes

Servings:

- Number of servings: 4

Nutrition Information (per serving):

- Calories: approximately 450 kcal
- Protein: 30 g

- Fat: 22 g
- Carbohydrates: 35 g
- Fiber: 7 g
- Sugar: 3 g

SALAD WITH QUAIL EGGS, SMOKED SALMON, AND CHERRY TOMATOES

Ingredients:

- 4 quail eggs
- 4 oz (115g) smoked salmon, thinly sliced
- 1 cup cherry tomatoes, halved
- 4 cups mixed salad greens
- 1 tablespoon capers, drained
- 1/4 red onion, thinly sliced
- Fresh dill, chopped, for garnish (optional)

For the Dressing:

- 2 tablespoons olive oil
- 1 tablespoon lemon juice
- 1 teaspoon Dijon mustard
- Salt and pepper to taste

Directions:

1. Prepare the Quail Eggs:

- Bring a small pot of water to a boil.
- Gently drop the quail eggs into the hot water.
- Boil for 2-3 minutes for soft-boiled eggs or 4-5 minutes for hard-boiled eggs.

- Take the eggs out of the boiling water and let them cool in a bowl of ice water.
- Once cooled, peel the eggs and slice them in half.

2. *Assemble the Salad:*

- In a large salad bowl, arrange mixed salad greens.
- Top with sliced smoked salmon, halved cherry tomatoes, red onion, and capers.
- Arrange quail egg halves on top of the salad.

3. *Make the Dressing:*

- Combine the olive oil, lemon juice, Dijon mustard, salt, and pepper in a small bowl.

4. *Serve:*

- Drizzle the salad with the dressing.
- Garnish with chopped fresh dill, if desired.

Prep Time:

- Preparation: 10 minutes
- Cooking (for quail eggs): 5 minutes
- Total: 15 minutes

Servings:

- Number of servings: 2

Nutrition Information (per serving):

- Calories: approximately 300 kcal
- Protein: 20 g
- Fat: 20 g
- Carbohydrates: 10 g
- Fiber: 3 g
- Sugar: 4 g

SHRIMP SALAD WITH MELON, WATERMELON, AND ARUGULA

Ingredients:

- 1 lb (450g) shrimp, peeled and deveined
- Salt and pepper to taste
- 1 tablespoon olive oil
- 4 cups arugula (rocket), washed and dried
- 1 cup cubed honeydew melon
- 1 cup cubed watermelon
- 1/2 cup crumbled feta cheese
- 1/4 cup fresh mint leaves, chopped

For the Dressing:

- 3 tablespoons olive oil
- 2 tablespoons lemon juice
- 1 teaspoon honey
- Salt and pepper to taste

Directions:

1. Cook the Shrimp:

- Season shrimp with salt and pepper.
- In a big skillet, warm up the olive oil over medium-high heat.

- Add the shrimp to the skillet and cook until pink and opaque, 2 to 3 minutes per side.
- Remove from heat and set aside to cool slightly.

2. Prepare the Salad:

- In a large salad bowl, combine arugula, cubed honeydew melon, cubed watermelon, crumbled feta cheese, and chopped mint leaves.

3. Make the Dressing:

- In a small bowl, thoroughly mix olive oil, lemon juice, honey, salt, and pepper.

4. Assemble the Salad:

- Add cooked shrimp to the salad bowl with the other ingredients.
- Drizzle the dressing over the salad and toss gently to combine.

5. Serve:

- Divide the salad onto serving plates.
- Serve immediately and enjoy!

Prep Time:

- Preparation: 15 minutes
- Cooking (for shrimp): 5 minutes
- Total: 20 minutes

Servings:

- Number of servings: 4

Nutrition Information (per serving):

- Calories: approximately 250 kcal
- Protein: 25 g
- Fat: 12 g
- Carbohydrates: 15 g
- Fiber: 2 g
- Sugar: 10 g

BEAN SALAD

Ingredients:

- 1 can (15 oz) kidney beans, drained and rinsed
- 1 can (15 oz) cannellini beans, drained and rinsed
- 1 can (15 oz) black beans, drained and rinsed
- 1 red bell pepper, diced
- 1/2 red onion, finely chopped
- 1/4 cup chopped fresh parsley
- 1/4 cup chopped fresh cilantro
- 1/4 cup olive oil
- 2 tablespoons red wine vinegar
- 1 teaspoon Dijon mustard
- Salt and pepper to taste

Directions:

1. Prepare the Beans:

- Rinse and drain kidney beans, cannellini beans, and black beans thoroughly.

2. Mix the Salad:

- In a large mixing bowl, mix together the rinsed beans, diced red bell pepper, finely chopped red onion, chopped fresh parsley, and chopped fresh cilantro.

3. Make the Dressing:

- Whisk together olive oil, red wine vinegar, Dijon mustard, salt, and pepper in a small bowl until well combined.

4. Combine and Serve:

- Pour the dressing over the bean mixture into the large bowl.
- Toss gently to coat all ingredients evenly with the dressing.

5. Chill and Serve:

- To enable the flavors to mingle, cover and chill the salad for at least an hour before serving.

6. Serve:

- Serve chilled as a side dish or a light main dish.
- Optionally, garnish with additional fresh herbs before serving.

Prep Time:

- Preparation: 15 minutes
- Chilling: 1 hour
- Total: 1 hour 15 minutes

Servings:

- Number of servings: 6

Nutrition Information (per serving):

- Calories: approximately 250 kcal
- Protein: 10 g
- Fat: 10 g
- Carbohydrates: 30 g
- Fiber: 10 g
- Sugar: 2 g

TUNA AND CAPER SALAD

Ingredients:

- Two drained 5-ounce cans of tuna each in water
- 1/4 cup capers, drained and rinsed
- 1/2 red onion, thinly sliced
- 1 cucumber, diced
- 1 cup cherry tomatoes, halved
- 1/4 cup Kalamata olives, sliced
- 1/4 cup fresh parsley, chopped
- 2 tablespoons extra virgin olive oil
- 1 tablespoon lemon juice
- Salt and pepper to taste
- Mixed salad greens (optional for serving)

Directions:

1. Prepare the Salad Base:
- Combine drained tuna, capers, thinly sliced red onion, diced cucumber, halved cherry tomatoes, and sliced Kalamata olives, and add freshly cut parsley to a big bowl.

2. Make the Dressing:
- In a small bowl, whisk together lemon juice, extra virgin olive oil, salt, and pepper.

3. Combine and Toss:
- Transfer the tuna and vegetable combination to a large bowl and cover with the dressing.

- Gently toss everything together until the dressing is thoroughly distributed and well blended.

4. Serve:

- Present the tuna and caper salad right away, either by itself or, if preferred, on top of a bed of mixed salad greens.

Prep Time:

- Preparation: 15 minutes
- Total: 15 minutes

Servings:

- Number of servings: 4

Nutrition Information (per serving):

- Calories: approximately 250 kcal
- Protein: 25 g
- Fat: 12 g
- Carbohydrates: 10 g
- Fiber: 3 g
- Sugar: 4 g

AVOCADO AND CRAB SALAD WITH PINE NUT DRESSING

Ingredients:

- 2 ripe avocados, peeled, pitted, and diced
- 1 cup crab meat, cooked and shredded
- 1/4 cup pine nuts, toasted
- 1/4 cup fresh cilantro, chopped
- 1/4 cup red bell pepper, diced
- 2 tablespoons red onion, finely chopped
- Juice of 1 lemon
- Salt and pepper to taste
- Mixed salad greens (optional for serving)

For the Pine Nut Dressing:

- 1/4 cup pine nuts, toasted
- 1/4 cup extra virgin olive oil
- 2 tablespoons lemon juice
- One tablespoon of maple syrup or honey, if desired, for sweetness
- Salt and pepper to taste

Directions:

1. Prepare the Salad:

- Combine diced avocado, cooked and shredded crab meat, toasted pine nuts, chopped cilantro, diced red bell pepper, and finely chopped red onion in a large bowl.

2. Make the Pine Nut Dressing:

- Place the toasted pine nuts, extra virgin olive oil, lemon juice, honey or maple syrup (if desired), salt, and pepper in a blender or food processor.
- Blend till creamy and smooth. Taste and adjust the seasoning.

3. Assemble the Salad:

- Drizzle the pine nut dressing in the bowl over the avocado and crab mixture.
- Gently toss everything together until the dressing is thoroughly distributed and well blended.

4. Serve:

- Present the avocado and crab salad right away, either by itself or, if preferred, on a bed of mixed salad greens.
- Optionally, garnish with additional toasted pine nuts and cilantro.

Prep Time:

- Preparation: 15 minutes
- Total: 15 minutes

Servings:

- Number of servings: 4

Nutrition Information (per serving):

- Calories: approximately 300 kcal
- Protein: 10 g
- Fat: 25 g
- Carbohydrates: 15 g
- Fiber: 7 g
- Sugar: 3 g

QUINOA AND FETA VEGETABLE SALAD

Ingredients:

- 1 cup quinoa, rinsed
- 2 cups water or vegetable broth
- 1 red bell pepper, diced
- 1 yellow bell pepper, diced
- 1 cucumber, diced
- 1 cup cherry tomatoes, halved
- 1/2 cup red onion, finely chopped
- 1/2 cup Kalamata olives, sliced
- 1/2 cup crumbled feta cheese
- 1/4 cup fresh parsley, chopped
- 1/4 cup fresh mint leaves, chopped

For the Dressing:

- 1/4 cup olive oil
- 2 tablespoons lemon juice
- 1 clove garlic, minced
- 1 teaspoon Dijon mustard
- Salt and pepper to taste

Directions:

1. Cook Quinoa:

- In a saucepan, bring water or vegetable broth to a boil.

- Add quinoa, reduce heat to low, cover, and simmer for 15 minutes or until liquid is absorbed and quinoa is tender.
- Turn off the heat and leave it covered for five minutes. Fluff with a fork and let cool.

2. Prepare Vegetables:

- In a sizable bowl, mix chopped red and yellow bell peppers, cucumbers, cherry tomatoes, red onion, and Kalamata olives.

3. Make the Dressing:

- Mix olive oil, lemon juice, minced garlic, Dijon mustard, salt, and pepper.

4. Assemble the Salad:

- Transfer the cooled quinoa to the veggie bowl.
- Pour the dressing over the salad and toss gently to combine.

5. Add Feta and Herbs:

- Gently fold in crumbled feta cheese, chopped fresh parsley, and chopped fresh mint leaves.

6. Serve:

- To let the flavors mingle, serve the salad right away or chill it for at least half an hour.
- Garnish with additional herbs or feta cheese if desired.

Prep Time:

- Preparation: 15 minutes
- Cooking: 15 minutes
- Total: 30 minutes

Servings:

- Number of servings: 4

Nutrition Information (per serving):

- Calories: approximately 350 kcal
- Protein: 10 g
- Fat: 18 g
- Carbohydrates: 35 g
- Fiber: 6 g
- Sugar: 5 g

WARM MEDITERRANEAN LAMB SALAD

Ingredients:

- 1 lb (450g) lamb leg steaks, thinly sliced
- Salt and pepper to taste
- 2 tablespoons olive oil
- 1 teaspoon dried oregano
- 1 teaspoon dried thyme
- 1 teaspoon paprika
- 1 cucumber, diced
- 1 cup cherry tomatoes, halved
- 1/2 red onion, thinly sliced
- 1/2 cup Kalamata olives, pitted and halved
- 1/4 cup crumbled feta cheese
- Juice of 1 lemon
- 2 tablespoons extra virgin olive oil
- Mint leaves, chopped (for garnish)

Directions:

1. Prepare the Lamb:

- Season the lamb slices with salt, pepper, oregano, thyme, and paprika.

2. Cook the Lamb:

- In a big skillet, warm up the olive oil over medium-high heat. Add the seasoned lamb slices and cook for 3-4 minutes per side or until browned and cooked to your liking (medium-rare to medium).

3. Prepare the Salad:

- Combine diced cucumber, cherry tomatoes, thinly sliced red onion, Kalamata olives, and crumbled feta cheese in a large salad bowl.

4. Make the Dressing:

- Whisk lemon juice and extra virgin olive oil in a small bowl—season with salt and pepper to taste.

5. Combine and Serve:

- Add the cooked lamb slices to the salad bowl. Pour the dressing over the salad and lamb.
- Toss gently to combine, ensuring the lamb and vegetables are coated with the dressing.

6. Garnish and Serve:

- Sprinkle chopped fresh parsley or mint leaves over the salad.
- Serve warm immediately.

Prep Time:

- Preparation: 15 minutes
- Cooking: 10 minutes
- Total: 25 minutes

Servings:

- Number of servings: 4

Nutrition Information (per serving):

- Calories: approximately 380 kcal
- Protein: 28 g
- Fat: 26 g
- Carbohydrates: 10 g
- Fiber: 3 g
- Sugar: 5 g

CHICKEN SPINACH SOUP

Ingredients:

- 1 tablespoon olive oil
- 1 onion, chopped
- 2 carrots, diced
- 2 celery stalks, diced
- 2 cloves garlic, minced
- 4 cups chicken broth
- two cups cooked chicken breast, diced or shredded
- 4 cups fresh spinach leaves, chopped
- 1 teaspoon dried thyme
- Salt and pepper to taste
- Lemon wedges for serving (optional)

Directions:

1. Sauté the Vegetables:

- Heat olive oil in a large pot over medium heat.
- Add chopped onion, diced carrots, and diced celery.
- Sauté for 5-7 minutes until the vegetables are softened and onions are translucent.
- Add minced garlic and sauté for another 1-2 minutes until fragrant.

2. Add Broth and Simmer:

- Pour in chicken broth and bring to a boil.
- Reduce heat to low and simmer for 10-15 minutes or until the carrots are tender.

3. Add Chicken and Spinach:

- Stir in cooked chicken breast and chopped spinach leaves.
- Season with salt, pepper, and dry thyme.
- Sauté until the chicken is heated through and the spinach has wilted, about 5 more minutes.

4. Serve:

- Ladle the soup into bowls.
- Optionally, squeeze a lemon wedge over each serving for freshness.
- Serve hot and enjoy!

Prep Time:

- Preparation: 10 minutes
- Cooking: 25 minutes
- Total: 35 minutes

Servings:

- Number of servings: 4

Nutrition Information (per serving):

- Calories: approximately 200 kcal
- Protein: 20 g
- Fat: 7 g
- Carbohydrates: 15 g
- Fiber: 4 g
- Sugar: 5 g

CHEESY SHRIMP AND HERB SOUP

Ingredients:

- 1 tablespoon butter
- 1 onion, finely chopped
- 2 cloves garlic, minced
- 2 tablespoons all-purpose flour
- 3 cups chicken or vegetable broth
- 1 cup milk (or half-and-half for a more decadent soup)
- 1 cup shredded cheddar cheese
- 1 cup cooked shrimp, peeled and deveined
- One cup mixed fresh herbs (parsley, dill, and chives), chopped
- Salt and pepper to taste
- Optional: crusty bread for serving

Directions:

1. *Sauté the Aromatics:*

- Melt butter in a big pot over a medium heat.
- Add chopped onion and minced garlic. Sauté for 3-4 minutes until onion is translucent and fragrant.

2. Make the Roux:

- Dust the onion and garlic mixture with flour. For one to two minutes, stir continuously to cook the flour and make a roux.

3. Add Broth and Simmer:

- Add the chicken or vegetable broth gradually, stirring continuously to prevent lumps.
- After bringing the mixture to a boil, turn down the heat. Simmer until the soup thickens slightly, stirring regularly, for ten minutes.

4. Add Milk and Cheese:

- Stir in milk (or half-and-half) and shredded cheddar cheese. Stir the soup continuously until the cheese melts and is mixed in.

5. Add Shrimp and Herbs:

- Add cooked shrimp to the soup. Simmer gently for 2-3 minutes until the shrimp are heated through.

6. Season and Serve:

- Stir in chopped fresh herbs (parsley, dill, and chives).
- Season with salt and pepper to taste.

7. Serve:

- Ladle the soup into bowls.
- Optionally, serve with crusty bread for dipping.

Prep Time:

- Preparation: 10 minutes
- Cooking: 20 minutes
- Total: 30 minutes

Servings:

- Number of servings: 4

Nutrition Information (per serving):

- Calories: approximately 300 kcal
- Protein: 20 g
- Fat: 18 g
- Carbohydrates: 15 g
- Fiber: 1 g
- Sugar: 5 g

CHICKPEA SOUP WITH CALAMARI

Ingredients:

- 1 cup dried chickpeas, soaked overnight (or 2 cans, drained and rinsed)
- 1 lb (450g) calamari (squid), cleaned and sliced into rings
- 1 onion, chopped
- 2 cloves garlic, minced
- 2 tablespoons olive oil
- 1 carrot, diced
- 1 celery stalk, diced
- 1 bay leaf
- 1 teaspoon paprika
- 1/2 teaspoon ground cumin
- 1/2 teaspoon dried thyme
- 4 cups vegetable or chicken broth
- Salt and pepper to taste
- Fresh parsley, chopped, for garnish
- Lemon wedges for serving

Directions:

1. Prepare the Chickpeas:

- If using dried chickpeas, drain and rinse them after soaking overnight. If using canned chickpeas, drain and rinse them as well.

2. Sauté Aromatics:

- Heat olive oil in a large pot over medium heat.

- Add chopped onion, minced garlic, diced carrot, and diced celery. Sauté for 5-7 minutes until vegetables are softened.

3. Add Spices and Herbs:

- Stir in bay leaf, paprika, ground cumin, and dried thyme. Cook for 1 minute until fragrant.

4. Cook the Soup:

- Add soaked (or canned) chickpeas to the pot.
- Pour in vegetable or chicken broth. Bring to a boil, then reduce heat to low. Simmer uncovered for 30-40 minutes or until chickpeas are tender.

5. Prepare the Calamari:

- While the soup is simmering, prepare the calamari.
- Heat a separate skillet over medium-high heat. Add a little olive oil if needed.
- Add sliced calamari rings to the skillet and cook for 2-3 minutes until just opaque and tender—season with salt and pepper.

6. Combine and Serve:

- Add cooked calamari to the chickpea soup. Stir gently to combine.
- Season with salt and pepper to taste.
- Remove the bay leaf from the soup.

7. Serve:

- Ladle the soup into bowls.
- Garnish with chopped fresh parsley.
- Serve hot with lemon wedges on the side.

Prep Time:

- Preparation: 15 minutes (plus soaking time for dried chickpeas)
- Cooking: 50 minutes
- Total: 1 hour 5 minutes

Servings:

- Number of servings: 4

Nutrition Information (per serving):

- Calories: approximately 300 kcal
- Protein: 25 g
- Fat: 8 g

- Carbohydrates: 35 g
- Fiber: 10 g
- Sugar: 5 g

PUMPKIN CREAM SOUP WITH SHRIMP

Ingredients:

- 1 small pumpkin (about 2 lbs or 1 kg), peeled, seeded, and diced
- 1 onion, chopped
- 2 cloves garlic, minced
- 4 cups vegetable or chicken broth
- 1 cup heavy cream
- 1/2 teaspoon ground nutmeg
- Salt and pepper to taste
- 1 lb (450g) shrimp, peeled and deveined
- 2 tablespoons olive oil
- Fresh parsley or chives, chopped, for garnish

Directions:

1. Prepare the Pumpkin:

- Peel, seed, and dice the pumpkin into small cubes.

2. Cook the Soup:

- In a large pot, heat olive oil over medium heat.
- Add chopped onion and minced garlic. Sauté for 3-4 minutes until onion is translucent.

3. Add Pumpkin and Broth:

- Add diced pumpkin to the pot.
- Add enough chicken or veggie broth to cover the pumpkin.

- Bring to a boil, then reduce heat to low. Cover and simmer for 20-25 minutes.

4. Blend the Soup:
- Remove the pot from heat. Use an immersion blender to purée the soup until smooth. Alternatively, carefully transfer the soup in batches to a blender and blend until smooth. Be cautious with hot liquids.

5. Add Cream and Seasoning:
- Return the puréed soup to the pot over low heat.
- Stir in heavy cream and ground nutmeg.
- Season with salt and pepper to taste. Simmer for another 5 minutes, stirring occasionally.

6. Cook the Shrimp:
- Heat the olive oil in a skillet over medium-high heat while the soup is boiling.
- Add the shrimp and cook for two to three minutes on each side or until they are cooked through and pink.

7. Serve:
- Ladle the hot soup into bowls.
- Top each serving with cooked shrimp.
- Garnish with chopped fresh parsley or chives.

Prep Time:
- Preparation: 15 minutes
- Cooking: 35-40 minutes
- Total: 50-55 minutes

Servings:
- Number of servings: 6

Nutrition Information (per serving):
- Calories: approximately 300 kcal
- Protein: 20 g
- Fat: 18 g
- Carbohydrates: 20 g
- Fiber: 4 g
- Sugar: 6 g

MEDITERRANEAN TOMATO SOUP WITH SQUID

Ingredients:

- 1 lb (450g) squid tubes, cleaned and sliced into rings
- 2 tablespoons olive oil
- 1 onion, finely chopped
- 2 cloves garlic, minced
- 1 carrot, diced
- 1 celery stalk, diced
- 1 red bell pepper, diced
- 1 yellow bell pepper, diced
- 1 can (14 oz or 400g) diced tomatoes
- 4 cups fish or vegetable broth
- 1 teaspoon dried thyme
- 1 teaspoon dried oregano
- Salt and pepper to taste
- Fresh basil leaves, chopped, for garnish

Directions:

1. Prepare the Squid:
- Clean the squid tubes by removing any skin and cartilage. Slice into rings and set aside.

2. Sauté Aromatics:
- In a big pot, warm the olive oil over medium heat.

- Add chopped onion and minced garlic. Sauté for 2-3 minutes until fragrant and onions are translucent.

3. Add Vegetables:

- Stir in diced carrot, celery, red bell pepper, and yellow bell pepper. Cook for 7 minutes until vegetables begin to soften.

4. Simmer with Tomatoes and Broth:

- Add diced tomatoes to the pot.
- Pour in fish or vegetable broth.
- Stir in dried thyme and dried oregano.
- Season with salt and pepper to taste.

5. Cook the Soup:

- After bringing the mixture to a boil, turn down the heat.
- Cover and simmer for 15-19 minutes, stirring occasionally, until vegetables are tender.

6. Add Squid:

- Add the sliced squid rings to the pot.
- Simmer for 5-7 minutes or until squid is opaque and cooked through.

7. Serve:

- Remove the pot from heat.
- Ladle the hot soup into bowls.
- Garnish with chopped fresh basil leaves.
- Serve hot and enjoy!

Prep Time:

- Preparation: 15 minutes
- Cooking: 30 minutes
- Total: 45 minutes

Servings:

- Number of servings: 4

Nutrition Information (per serving):

- Calories: approximately 250 kcal
- Protein: 25 g
- Fat: 8 g

- Carbohydrates: 20 g
- Fiber: 5 g
- Sugar: 8 g

LIGHT SPINACH SOUP PUREE

Ingredients:

- 1 tablespoon olive oil
- 1 onion, chopped
- 2 cloves garlic, minced
- 1 potato, peeled and diced
- 4 cups vegetable broth
- 1 lb (450g) fresh spinach, washed and trimmed
- Salt and pepper to taste
- 1/2 cup heavy cream
- Fresh lemon juice (optional for serving)

Directions:

1. Sauté Vegetables:

- Heat olive oil over medium heat. Add chopped onion and garlic, and sauté until softened and fragrant, about 3-4 minutes.

2. Add Potato and Broth:

- Add diced potato to the pot and pour in vegetable broth. When the water reaches a boil, turn down the heat and cook the potato gently for ten minutes or until it is soft.

3. Add Spinach:

- Add the fresh spinach, stir, and cook until wilted, 2 to 3 minutes.

4. Blend the Soup:

- Remove the pot from heat. Use an immersion blender to blend the soup until smooth. Alternatively, carefully transfer the soup in batches to a blender and blend until smooth.

5. Season and Finish:

- Season the soup with salt and pepper to taste.
- If using, stir in heavy cream or coconut milk for a creamier texture.

6. Serve:

- Ladle the spinach soup into bowls. If preferred, drizzle each plate with a little freshly squeezed lemon juice.
- Garnish with a sprinkle of black pepper or olive oil, if desired.

Prep Time:

- Preparation: 10 minutes
- Cooking: 20 minutes
- Total: 30 minutes

Servings:

- Number of servings: 4

Nutrition Information (per serving, without optional ingredients):

- Calories: approximately 120 kcal
- Protein: 4 g
- Fat: 5 g
- Carbohydrates: 17 g
- Fiber: 4 g
- Sugar: 3 g

MUSSEL SOUP

Ingredients:

- 2 pounds (900g) mussels, cleaned and debearded
- 2 tablespoons olive oil
- 1 onion, finely chopped
- 2 cloves garlic, minced
- 1 celery stalk, diced
- 1 carrot, diced
- 1 potato, peeled and diced
- 1 bay leaf
- 1 teaspoon dried thyme (or 1 tablespoon fresh thyme leaves)
- 1/2 cup dry white wine
- 4 cups fish or vegetable broth
- 1 cup canned diced tomatoes
- Salt and pepper to taste
- Fresh parsley, chopped (for garnish)
- Crusty bread (optional for serving)

Directions:

1. Prepare the Mussels:

- Use cold running water to scrub the mussels to get rid of any dirt and, if needed, debeard them. Discard any mussels that are open and do not close when tapped.

2. *Sauté Vegetables:*

- Heat olive oil over medium heat. Add chopped onion, minced garlic, celery, carrot, and potato. Sauté for 5-7 minutes until the vegetables are softened.

3. *Add Seasonings and Liquids:*

- Stir in bay leaf and dried thyme (or fresh thyme leaves). Pour in dry white wine and cook for 2-3 minutes to allow the alcohol to evaporate.
- Add fish or vegetable broth and diced tomatoes. Once it reaches a boil, reduce the heat and let the vegetables gently cook for ten minutes or until they become tender.

4. *Cook the Mussels:*

- Add cleaned mussels to the pot. Cook, covered, until all of the mussels have opened, shaking the pot once or twice during that time. Discard any mussels that do not open.

5. *Season and Serve:*

- Season the soup with salt and pepper to taste. Remove the bay leaf.
- Ladle the mussel soup into bowls. Garnish with chopped fresh parsley.
- Serve hot, optionally, with crusty bread on the side.

Prep Time:

- Preparation: 20 minutes
- Cooking: 25 minutes
- Total: 45 minutes

Servings:

- Number of servings: 4

Nutrition Information (per serving):

- Calories: approximately 300 kcal
- Protein: 25 g
- Fat: 10 g
- Carbohydrates: 20 g
- Fiber: 3 g
- Sugar: 5 g

SALMON IN CURRY BROTH

Ingredients:

- 4 salmon fillets, about 6 oz (170g) each
- Salt and pepper to taste
- 1 tablespoon olive oil
- 1 onion, finely chopped
- 2 cloves garlic, minced
- 1 tablespoon curry powder
- 1/2 teaspoon ground turmeric
- 1/2 teaspoon ground cumin
- 1/2 teaspoon ground coriander
- 4 cups fish or vegetable broth
- 1 can (14 oz / 400ml) coconut milk
- Juice of 1 lime
- Fresh cilantro, chopped (for garnish)
- Cooked rice or crusty bread (for serving)

Directions:

1. Prepare the Salmon:

- Pat dry the salmon fillets with paper towels—season both sides with salt and pepper.

2. Sear the Salmon:

- Heat in a large skillet of olive oil over medium-high heat. Place salmon fillets in the skillet, skin side down if skin-on, and cook for 3-4 minutes until browned and crispy.

Turn the fillets over and cook for a further three to four minutes or until the salmon reaches the desired doneness. Take out the salmon and place it aside from the skillet.

3. Make the Curry Broth:

- In the same skillet or pot, add chopped onion and sauté for 3-4 minutes until softened. Add minced garlic, curry powder, turmeric, cumin, and coriander. Cook for 1 minute until fragrant.

4. Simmer the Broth:

- Pour in fish or vegetable broth and bring to a simmer. After adding the coconut milk, simulate for an additional six minutes to let the flavors combine.

5. Finish and Serve:

- Return the seared salmon fillets to the skillet with the curry broth. Simmer for another 2-3 minutes to heat through.
- Squeeze lime juice over the salmon and curry broth. Adjust seasoning with salt and pepper.

6. Serve:

- Divide the salmon and curry broth among serving bowls. Garnish with chopped fresh cilantro.
- Serve hot, accompanied with cooked rice or crusty bread.

Prep Time:

- Preparation: 10 minutes
- Cooking: 20 minutes
- Total: 30 minutes

Servings:

- Number of servings: 4

Nutrition Information (per serving, without rice or bread):

- Calories: approximately 400 kcal
- Protein: 30 g
- Fat: 30 g
- Carbohydrates: 10 g
- Fiber: 2 g
- Sugar: 2 g

CHILLED TOMATO SOUP WITH BASIL

Ingredients:

- 2 lbs (about 900g) ripe tomatoes, chopped
- 1 cucumber, peeled, seeded, and chopped
- 1 red bell pepper, seeded and chopped
- 1 small red onion, chopped
- 2 cloves garlic, minced
- 3 cups tomato juice or vegetable broth
- 1/4 cup extra virgin olive oil
- Two tablespoons of red wine vinegar
- 1/4 cup fresh basil leaves, chopped
- Salt and pepper to taste
- Optional garnishes: extra basil leaves, drizzle of olive oil, croutons

Directions:

1. Prepare the Vegetables:

- In a big bowl, mix chopped tomatoes, cucumber, red onion, red bell pepper, and minced garlic.

2. Blend the Soup:

- Transfer the vegetable mixture to a food processor or blender, working in batches. Add tomato juice or vegetable broth.
- Blend until smooth and well combined.

3. Season and Chill:

- Pour the blended soup into a large bowl. Add chopped basil, red wine vinegar (or balsamic vinegar), and extra virgin olive oil. Season with salt and pepper to taste.

4. Chill:

- Place plastic wrap over the bowl and chill it in the refrigerator for at least two hours or until it is very cold.

5. Serve:

- Stir the chilled soup before serving. Ladle into bowls.
- If wanted, garnish with croutons, extra basil leaves, and a drizzle of olive oil.

Prep Time:

- Preparation: 20 minutes
- Chilling: 2 hours
- Total: 2 hours 20 minutes

Servings:

- Number of servings: 6

Nutrition Information (per serving):

- Calories: approximately 150 kcal
- Protein: 3 g
- Fat: 10 g
- Carbohydrates: 15 g
- Fiber: 4 g
- Sugar: 9 g

CHAPTER 2 : MA`IN COURSES WITH FISH, MEAT, AND VEGETABLES

SIDE DISHES AND SAUCES

COD WITH TOMATOES

Ingredients:

- 4 cod fillets (about 6 oz each), fresh or thawed if frozen
- 2 tablespoons olive oil
- 2 cloves garlic, minced
- 1 onion, thinly sliced
- 2 cups cherry tomatoes, halved
- 1/2 cup white wine or chicken broth
- 1 tablespoon tomato paste
- 1 teaspoon dried oregano
- Salt and pepper to taste
- Fresh parsley, chopped (optional for garnish)
- Lemon wedges (optional for serving)

Directions:

1. Season the cod fillets with salt and pepper.
2. Heat the olive oil in a big skillet over medium heat.
3. Fill the skillet with finely sliced onion and minced garlic. Sauté for 2-3 minutes until the onion starts to soften.
4. When the cherry tomatoes start to lose their juices, add them to the skillet and simmer for two to three minutes.
5. Stir in white wine or chicken broth, tomato paste, and dried oregano. Bring to a simmer.

6. Place the cod fillets into the skillet, spooning some of the tomato mixture over the top.
7. Cover the skillet with a lid and simmer gently for about 8-10 minutes, or until the cod is cooked and flakes easily with a fork.
8. Turn off the heat and, if desired, sprinkle chopped parsley on top of the skillet.
9. Serve the cod with the tomato mixture spooned over the top.
10. Optionally, serve with lemon wedges on the side for squeezing over the fish.

Prep Time:

- Preparation: 10 minutes
- Cooking: 15 minutes
- Total: 25 minutes

Servings:

- Number of servings: 4

Nutrition Information (per serving):

- Calories: approximately 250 kcal
- Protein: 30 g
- Fat: 10 g
- Carbohydrates: 8 g
- Fiber: 2 g
- Sugar: 4 g

SPAGHETTI WITH SHRIMP AND PISTACHIOS

Ingredients:

- 8 oz spaghetti
- 1/2 lb shrimp, peeled and deveined
- 2 tablespoons olive oil
- 2 cloves garlic, minced
- 1/4 cup pistachios, shelled and chopped
- 1/4 cup fresh parsley, chopped
- Zest of 1 lemon
- Juice of 1/2 lemon
- Salt and pepper to taste
- Grated Parmesan cheese for serving (optional)

Directions:

1. Cook the pasta until al dente. After draining, set away.
2. Heat the olive oil in a skillet over medium heat while the spaghetti cooks.
3. Add the minced garlic to the pan and cook it until fragrant, about one minute.
4. Add the shrimp to the skillet and cook for two to three minutes on each side or until they are opaque and pink.
5. Stir in chopped pistachios, parsley, lemon zest, and lemon juice. Cook for another 1-2 minutes until heated through.
6. Season with salt and pepper to taste.
7. Include the cooked spaghetti in the skillet and toss well to distribute the shrimp mixture throughout.

8. Remove from heat and serve immediately.
9. Optionally, garnish with grated Parmesan cheese before serving.

Prep Time:

- Preparation: 10 minutes
- Cooking: 15 minutes
- Total: 25 minutes

Servings:

- Number of servings: 2-3

Nutrition Information (per serving):

- Calories: approximately 400 kcal
- Protein: 25 g
- Fat: 15 g
- Carbohydrates: 40 g
- Fiber: 4 g
- Sugar: 2 g

PASTA WITH SPINACH AND SALMON

Ingredients:

- 8 oz pasta (such as spaghetti or fettuccine)
- 1 lb salmon fillet, skinless and boneless, cut into cubes
- 2 tablespoons olive oil
- 2 cloves garlic, minced
- 4 cups fresh spinach leaves
- 1/2 cup heavy cream or half-and-half
- 1/4 cup grated Parmesan cheese
- Salt and pepper to taste
- Crushed red pepper flakes (optional for heat)
- Fresh parsley, chopped (optional for garnish)
- Lemon wedges (optional for serving)

Directions:

1. Cook the Pasta:

- Bring a saucepan of salted water to a boil and cook the pasta until al dente. Pour out and set aside.

2. Prepare the Salmon and Spinach:

- Warm up some olive oil in a large skillet on a medium heat.
- Gently add the minced garlic to the skillet and cook it until fragrant, about one minute.
- Add cubed salmon to the skillet and cook for 3-4 minutes, stirring occasionally, until salmon is lightly browned and cooked.

- Boil the fresh spinach leaves in the skillet for one to two minutes or until they have wilted.

3. Combine and Finish:

- Pour heavy cream or half-and-half into the skillet with the salmon and spinach. Stir well and bring to a simmer.
- Add cooked pasta and grated Parmesan cheese to the skillet. Toss everything together until the pasta is well-coated and heated through.
- Season to taste with salt and pepper

4. Serve:

- Divide the pasta with salmon and spinach among serving plates.
- Garnish with chopped fresh parsley, if desired.
- Serve with lemon wedges on the side

Prep Time:

- Preparation: 10 minutes
- Cooking: 20 minutes
- Total: 30 minutes

Servings:

- Number of servings: 4

Nutrition Information (per serving):

- Calories: approximately 500 kcal
- Protein: 30 g
- Fat: 22 g
- Carbohydrates: 40 g
- Fiber: 3 g
- Sugar: 2 g

BAKED BEETROOT WITH BROWN RICE AND MOZZARELLA

Ingredients:

- 4 medium beetroots, trimmed and scrubbed
- 1 cup brown rice, rinsed
- 2 cups vegetable broth or water
- 1 tablespoon olive oil
- 1 onion, finely chopped
- Two cloves garlic, minced
- One teaspoon of dried thyme
- Salt and pepper to taste
- 1 cup shredded mozzarella cheese
- Fresh parsley, chopped (optional for garnish)

Directions:

1. Prepare the Beetroots:

- Preheat your oven to 400°F (200°C).
- Spread aluminum foil over each beetroot and arrange on a baking pan.
- Roast for 45 to 60 minutes, or until a fork inserted into the beetroots pierces them soft, in a preheated oven. Remove from the oven and let them cool slightly.

2. Cook the Brown Rice:

- While the beetroots are roasting, prepare the brown rice.

- In a medium-sized pot, warm the olive oil over medium heat.
- Add finely chopped onion and sauté for 3-4 minutes until translucent.
- Add minced garlic, and dried thyme, and sauté for another 1-2 minutes until fragrant.
- Stir in rinsed brown rice and cook for 1 minute to toast the rice slightly.
- Pour in some water or vegetable broth, bring to a boil, decrease the heat, cover, and simmer until the rice is tender and the liquid is absorbed around 40 to 45 minutes.

3. Assemble the Dish:

- Using your hands or a tiny knife, take off the beetroot skins once they are cold enough to handle. Cut them into circles.
- Arrange the sliced beetroots in a baking dish or individual oven-safe dishes.
- Spoon cooked brown rice evenly over the beetroot slices.
- After the rice and beetroot layers are cooked, top each with shredded mozzarella cheese.

4. Bake:

- Place the baking dish(es) in the oven and bake for 15-20 minutes or until the cheese is melted and bubbly.

5. Serve:

- Before serving, take it out of the oven and leave it cool for a few minutes.
- Garnish with chopped fresh parsley, if desired.
- Serve warm as a side dish or a light main course.

Prep Time:

- Preparation: 15 minutes
- Cooking (including roasting beetroots): 1 hour 15 minutes
- Total: 1 hour 30 minutes

Servings:

- Number of servings: 4

Nutrition Information (per serving):

- Calories: approximately 300 kcal
- Protein: 12 g
- Fat: 10 g
- Carbohydrates: 45 g
- Fiber: 6 g
- Sugar: 7 g

TURKEY BREAST WITH EGG AND CHEESE SAUCE

Ingredients:

- 4 turkey breast fillets (about 6 oz each)
- Salt and pepper to taste
- 2 tablespoons olive oil
- 2 tablespoons butter
- 2 tablespoons all-purpose flour
- 1 cup milk
- 1 cup shredded cheese (such as cheddar or mozzarella)
- 2 hard-boiled eggs, peeled and chopped
- Two tablespoons chopped fresh parsley (optional for garnish)

Directions:

1. Prepare the Turkey Breast:

- Season both sides of the turkey breast fillets with salt and pepper.
- Heat olive oil in a large skillet over medium-high heat.
- Add the turkey breast fillets to the skillet and cook for about 4-5 minutes per side or until golden brown and cooked through. Remove from heat and set aside.

2. Prepare the Sauce:

- In the same skillet, reduce heat to medium-low and add butter.
- After melting, add flour and whisk constantly for one to two minutes or until the mixture becomes fragrant and gently golden.
- Pour in the milk gradually, stirring continuously to avoid lumps.
- Cook the sauce for 3-4 minutes until thickened, stirring frequently.

- Stir in shredded cheese until melted and smooth.
- Add chopped hard-boiled eggs to the sauce and stir gently to combine. Cook for another 1-2 minutes until heated through.

3. Serve:

- Place the cooked turkey breast fillets on serving plates.
- Spoon the egg and cheese sauce over the turkey.
- Garnish with chopped fresh parsley, if using.
- Serve immediately, optionally, with steamed vegetables or mashed potatoes.

Prep Time:

- Preparation: 10 minutes
- Cooking: 20 minutes
- Total: 30 minutes

Servings:

- Number of servings: 4

Nutrition Information (per serving):

- Calories: approximately 400 kcal
- Protein: 35 g
- Fat: 22 g
- Carbohydrates: 12 g
- Fiber: 1 g
- Sugar: 3 g

PAN-SEARED SALMON WITH POACHED EGG, BROWN RICE, AND VEGETABLES

Ingredients:

- 4 salmon fillets (about 6 oz each), skin-on or skinless
- Salt and pepper to taste
- 1 tablespoon olive oil
- 4 eggs
- 1 cup brown rice, rinsed
- 2 cups water or vegetable broth
- Two cups mixed vegetables (such as bell peppers, zucchini, and carrots), diced
- 1 tablespoon butter
- 1 clove garlic, minced
- 1/4 cup of finely chopped fresh herbs (dill or parsley, for example)

Directions:

1. Prepare the Brown Rice:

- Bring two cups of water or vegetable broth to a boil in a medium saucepan.
- When the rice is soft and the liquid has been absorbed, add the rinsed brown rice, lower the heat to low, cover, and simmer for 40 to 45 minutes. After turning off the heat, leave it covered for five minutes and fluff with a fork before serving.

2. Cook the Vegetables:

- Heat the olive oil in a big pan over medium heat while the rice cooks.

- Add diced mixed vegetables to the skillet and sauté for 5-7 minutes, or until vegetables are tender-crisp—season with salt and pepper to taste. Remove from heat and set aside.

3. Prepare the Salmon:

- Use paper towels to pat dry the salmon fillets, then season both sides with salt and pepper.
- Place another big skillet on medium-high heat. Pour in some olive oil.
- Place salmon fillets in the skillet, skin-side down if using skin-on fillets, and cook for 4-5 minutes on each side or until the salmon is cooked. Remove from heat and set aside.

4. Poach the Eggs:

- While the salmon is cooking, poach the eggs. Bring a medium pot of water to a gentle simmer.
- Crack each egg into a small bowl or ramekin. Create a gentle whirlpool in the simmering water with a spoon and carefully slide the egg into the water. Poach for 3-4 minutes until the whites are set and yolks are still runny. Using a slotted spoon, remove and place on paper towels to drain.

5. Assemble the Dish:

- Divide cooked brown rice among serving plates.
- Top each plate with sautéed vegetables.
- Place a salmon fillet on top of the vegetables.
- Carefully place a poached egg on each salmon fillet.
- Optionally, garnish with chopped fresh herbs, such as parsley or dill.

6. Serve:

- Serve immediately while warm, optionally with lemon wedges for squeezing over the salmon.

Prep Time:

- Preparation: 15 minutes
- Cooking (for rice, vegetables, and salmon): 45 minutes
- Total: 60 minutes

Servings:

- Number of servings: 4

Nutrition Information (per serving):

- Calories: approximately 400 kcal
- Protein: 30 g
- Fat: 18 g
- Carbohydrates: 30 g
- Fiber: 4 g
- Sugar: 2 g

GRILLED LAMB WITH SALAD AND BAKED POTATO WITH EGG

Ingredients:

- 1 lb lamb chops or lamb loin chops
- Salt and pepper to taste
- 4 medium potatoes
- 4 eggs
- 2 tablespoons olive oil
- 4 cups mixed salad greens (lettuce, arugula, spinach, etc.)
- 1 cucumber, sliced
- 1 cup cherry tomatoes, halved
- 1/4 red onion, thinly sliced
- 1/4 cup crumbled feta cheese (optional)
- Fresh herbs (such as parsley or dill) for garnish

For the Marinade (optional):

- 2 tablespoons olive oil
- 2 cloves garlic, minced
- 1 teaspoon dried oregano
- Juice of 1 lemon
- Salt and pepper to taste

Directions:

1. Prepare the Lamb:

- If using the marinade, combine olive oil, minced garlic, dried oregano, lemon juice, salt, and pepper in a bowl. Coat the lamb chops evenly with the marinade and let them marinate in the refrigerator for at least 30 minutes.
- Turn the heat up to medium-high on the grill.
- Use salt and pepper to season the lamb chops.
- To get medium-rare, grill the lamb chops for 3-4 minutes on each side or until done. The thickness of the chops will determine how long they need to cook. Remove from the grill and let them rest for a few minutes before serving.

2. Prepare the Baked Potatoes:

- Preheat your oven to 400°F (200°C).
- Scrub the potatoes, clean them, and dry them with a paper towel.
- Prick each potato with a fork a few times.
- Toss the potatoes with salt and a thin coating of olive oil.
- Place the tasty potatoes on a baking sheet and bake for 45 to 60 minutes, or until a fork inserted into the potato comes out soft.

3. Prepare the Salad:

- Combine mixed salad greens, sliced cucumber, halved cherry tomatoes, and thinly sliced red onion in a large salad bowl.
- Top the salad with crumbled Greek feta cheese.

4. Prepare the Eggs:

- Boil a small saucepan of water while the potatoes are roasting.
- Place the eggs in the boiling water and cook for 7 minutes, or until the yolk is slightly runny and the whites are firm, depending on your desire.
- To make peeling eggs simpler, place the eggs in a dish of cold water to chill. After peeling, lay the eggs aside.

5. Assemble the Dish:

- Divide the mixed salad among serving plates.
- Place a grilled lamb chop on each plate.
- Cut each baked potato open lengthwise and place it on the plates.
- Cut each egg in half and place the baked potato halves on top.
- Garnish with fresh herbs, such as parsley or dill.

<u>*6. Serve:*</u>
- Serve warm, optionally, with a side of tzatziki sauce or your favorite condiment.

Prep Time:
- Preparation: 15 minutes (plus marinating time if using)
- Cooking (for potatoes and lamb): 60 minutes
- Total: 75 minutes (plus marinating time)

Servings:
- Number of servings: 4

Nutrition Information (per serving):
- Calories: approximately 500 kcal
- Protein: 30 g
- Fat: 25 g
- Carbohydrates: 35 g
- Fiber: 5 g
- Sugar: 4 g

CARBONARA PIZZA

Ingredients:

- 1 lb pizza dough, homemade or store-bought
- 1 cup grated mozzarella cheese
- 1/2 cup grated Parmesan cheese
- 4 slices bacon, cooked and chopped
- 2 large eggs
- 1/2 cup heavy cream
- 1/2 cup grated Pecorino Romano cheese
- 2 cloves garlic, minced
- Salt and black pepper to taste
- Fresh parsley, chopped (optional for garnish)
- Olive oil for drizzling

Directions:

1. Preheat the Oven:

- Preheat the oven to 475°F (245°C). To preheat the oven, place a baking sheet or pizza stone inside.

2. Prepare the Carbonara Sauce:

- Whisk together eggs, heavy cream, grated Pecorino Romano cheese, minced garlic, salt, and black pepper until well combined. Set aside.

3. Roll Out the Pizza Dough:

- On a surface dusted with flour, roll out the pizza dough to the required thickness for a circle or rectangle.

4. Assemble the Pizza:

- Transfer the rolled-out dough to a piece of parchment paper (if using a pizza stone) or directly onto a baking sheet.
- Drizzle olive oil over the dough and spread it evenly with your hands or a brush.
- Spread the grated mozzarella cheese evenly over the dough.
- Sprinkle the chopped bacon over the cheese.

5. Bake the Pizza:

- Carefully pour the carbonara sauce mixture over the pizza, spreading it evenly with the back of a spoon or spatula.
- Place the pizza on the baking sheet or pizza stone that has been warmed in the oven, using parchment paper if desired.
- Bake for 10 to 12 minutes, or until the cheese is bubbling and beginning to brown and the crust is golden brown.

6. Finish and Serve:

- Remove the pizza from the oven and let it cool for a few minutes.
- Sprinkle-grated Parmesan cheese over the hot pizza.
- Garnish with chopped fresh parsley, if desired.
- Slice and serve hot.

Prep Time:

- Preparation: 15 minutes
- Cooking: 10-12 minutes
- Total: 25-30 minutes

Servings:

- Number of servings: 4

Nutrition Information (per serving):

- Calories: approximately 500 kcal
- Protein: 22 g
- Fat: 28 g
- Carbohydrates: 40 g
- Fiber: 2 g
- Sugar: 2 g

FALAFEL WITH FETA, ONION, TOMATOES, HUMMUS, AND RICE

Ingredients:

- 1 cup dried chickpeas (garbanzo beans), soaked overnight
- 1 small onion, finely chopped
- 3 cloves garlic, minced
- 1/4 cup chopped fresh parsley
- 1/4 cup chopped fresh cilantro
- 1 teaspoon ground cumin
- 1 teaspoon ground coriander
- 1/2 teaspoon baking soda
- Salt and pepper to taste
- Vegetable oil for frying
- 1 cup crumbled feta cheese
- 1 small red onion, thinly sliced
- 1 cup cherry tomatoes, halved
- 1 cup hummus (store-bought or homemade)
- 2 cups cooked rice (white or brown)

For Serving (optional):

- Pita bread or wraps
- Fresh lettuce or salad greens
- Lemon wedges
- Tahini sauce or yogurt sauce

Directions:

1. Prepare the Falafel Mixture:

- Drain and rinse the soaked chickpeas. Pat them dry with paper towels.
- Combine chickpeas, chopped onion, minced garlic, parsley, cilantro, ground cumin, coriander, baking soda, salt, and pepper in a food processor.
- Pulse until the mixture is finely ground and holds together when squeezed. Avoid over-processing; it should be coarse and not completely smooth.

2. Shape and Fry the Falafel:

- Scoop tablespoon-sized portions of the falafel mixture and shape into small balls or patties using your hands.
- In a large skillet, heat the vegetable oil over medium-high heat.
- Gently drop the falafel into the heated oil and cook for 3-4 minutes on each side or until golden brown and crispy. To drain extra oil, transfer to a plate covered with paper towels.

3. Assemble the Dish:

- Divide the cooked rice among serving plates.
- Arrange the fried falafel on top of the rice.
- Scatter crumbled feta cheese, thinly sliced red onion, and halved cherry tomatoes around the falafel.

4. Serve:

- Serve with a dollop of hummus on the side or directly on the plate.
- Alternatively, serve with pita bread or wraps, fresh lettuce or salad greens, lemon wedges, tahini sauce, or yogurt sauce.

Prep Time:

- Preparation: 20 minutes (plus overnight soaking)
- Cooking: 15 minutes
- Total: 35 minutes (plus soaking time)

Servings:

- Number of servings: 4

Nutrition Information (per serving):

- Calories: approximately 500 kcal
- Protein: 20 g
- Fat: 20 g

- Carbohydrates: 60 g
- Fiber: 10 g
- Sugar: 5 g

CHICKEN WITH VEGETABLES AND SWEET POTATO FRIES

Ingredients:

- 4 boneless, skinless chicken breasts
- 2 sweet potatoes, peeled and cut into fries
- 2 tablespoons olive oil
- 1 teaspoon paprika
- 1 teaspoon garlic powder
- Salt and pepper to taste
- 1 teaspoon dried thyme (optional)
- 1 red bell pepper, sliced
- 1 yellow bell pepper, sliced
- 1 zucchini, sliced
- 1 red onion, sliced
- Fresh parsley or cilantro for garnish (optional)

For the Marinade (optional):

- Juice of 1 lemon
- 2 tablespoons olive oil
- 2 cloves garlic, minced
- 1 teaspoon dried oregano
- Salt and pepper to taste

Directions:

1. Prepare the Sweet Potato Fries:

- Set the oven temperature to 220 °C or 425°F.
- Place sweet potato fries in a big basin and toss to cover equally with 1 tablespoon olive oil, paprika, garlic powder, salt, pepper, and dried thyme, if using.
- Arrange the fries on a baking sheet covered with parchment paper.
- Bake for 21-26 minutes, flipping halfway through, until fries are golden and crispy. Remove from oven and set aside.

2. Prepare the Chicken:

- In a separate bowl, combine chicken breasts with the marinade ingredients (if using), or season with salt and pepper.
- Heat up one tablespoon of olive oil over medium-high heat in a pan.
- Add the chicken breasts and cook for 5 to 7 minutes on each side.
- Take out of the skillet and set aside.

3. Cook the Vegetables:

- Add sliced bell peppers, zucchini, and red onion in the same skillet.
- Sauté for 5-7 minutes or until vegetables are tender-crisp. Season with salt and pepper to taste.

4. Assemble the Dish:

- Slice the cooked chicken breasts.
- Divide sweet potato fries, sautéed vegetables, and sliced chicken breasts among serving plates.

5. Serve:

- Garnish with fresh parsley or cilantro, if desired.
- Serve hot and enjoy!

Prep Time:

- Preparation: 15 minutes
- Cooking (for sweet potato fries and chicken): 30 minutes
- Total: 45 minutes

Servings:

- Number of servings: 4

Nutrition Information (per serving):

- Calories: approximately 400 kcal
- Protein: 30 g
- Fat: 15 g
- Carbohydrates: 35 g
- Fiber: 7 g
- Sugar: 8 g

PASTA WITH SHRIMP

Ingredients:

- 8 oz (225g) pasta of your choice (linguine, spaghetti, or fettuccine)
- 1 lb (450g) shrimp, peeled and deveined
- 3 tablespoons olive oil
- 4 cloves garlic, minced
- 1/4 teaspoon red pepper flakes (optional)
- 1/2 cup dry white wine or chicken broth
- 1 cup cherry tomatoes, halved
- 1/4 cup fresh parsley, chopped
- Salt and pepper to taste
- Grated Parmesan cheese for serving
- Lemon wedges for serving (optional)

Directions:

1. Cook the Pasta:

- Start a big pot of water that has been salted and boiling.
- Cook the pasta following the directions on the box or until it is ready. After draining the pasta and reserving 1/2 cup of the water, set it aside.

2. Prepare the Shrimp:

- In a pan over medium-high heat, heat two tablespoons of olive oil while the pasta cooks.
- Add the shrimp to the skillet and cook for 2 to 3 minutes on each side or until they are pink and opaque. After taking the shrimp out of the pan, set it aside.

3. Make the Sauce:

- Add the last tablespoon of olive oil to the same skillet.
- Add the minced garlic and red pepper flakes, if using, and sauté until fragrant, about 1 minute.

4. Deglaze the Pan:

- Add the white wine or chicken broth, making sure to scrape off any remnants of browned food from the skillet's bottom. Cook for 2-3 minutes, allowing the liquid to reduce slightly.

5. Combine Pasta and Shrimp:

- Return the cooked shrimp to the skillet.
- Add the halved cherry tomatoes and chopped parsley.
- Season with salt and pepper to taste.

6. Finish the Dish:

- Toss the cooked pasta in the skillet to coat it evenly, adding a little of the leftover pasta water as required to loosen the sauce.

7. Serve:

- Divide the pasta with shrimp among serving plates.
- Sprinkle with grated Parmesan cheese.
- Serve with lemon wedges to squeeze over the pasta.

Prep Time:

- Preparation: 10 minutes
- Cooking: 20 minutes
- Total: 30 minutes

Servings:

- Number of servings: 4

Nutrition Information (per serving):

- Calories: approximately 400 kcal
- Protein: 30 g
- Fat: 12 g
- Carbohydrates: 40 g
- Fiber: 3 g
- Sugar: 3 g

BAKED DUCK BREAST

Ingredients:

- 2 duck breasts
- Salt and pepper to taste
- 1 tablespoon olive oil
- 2 cloves garlic, minced
- 1 teaspoon dried thyme
- 1 teaspoon dried rosemary
- 1/2 teaspoon paprika
- 1/2 teaspoon ground coriander
- 1/2 teaspoon ground cumin
- 1/4 cup dry white wine or chicken broth
- Fresh herbs (such as thyme or rosemary) for garnish (optional)

Directions:

1. Preheat the Oven:

- Warm your oven to 400°F (200°C).

2. Prepare the Duck Breasts:

- Using a sharp knife, score the duck breasts' skin in a crosshatch pattern, being cautious not to sever any flesh.
- Liberally season the duck breasts on both sides with salt and pepper.

3. Sear the Duck Breasts:

- In an oven-safe skillet, warm the olive oil over medium-high heat.

- Skin-side down put the duck breasts in the skillet. Sear for 5-7 minutes or until the skin is golden brown and crispy. Remove excess fat as it renders out.
- Turn the duck breasts over and sear the other side for 2-3 minutes.

4. Season and Bake:

- Take out of the skillet and place the duck breasts aside.
- Mix minced garlic, dried thyme, rosemary, paprika, ground coriander, and ground cumin in a small bowl.
- Rub the spice mixture evenly over the duck breasts.

5. Bake the Duck Breasts:

- Place the duck breasts back in the skillet, skin-side up.
- Pour white wine or chicken broth into the skillet around the duck breasts.
- Transfer the skillet to the preheated oven.
- Bake for 15-20 minutes to your desired doneness.

6. Rest and Serve:

- Take the duck breasts out of the oven, then give them five to ten minutes to rest before slicing.
- Slice the duck breasts diagonally and serve hot, garnished with fresh herbs if desired.

Prep Time:

- Preparation: 10 minutes
- Cooking: 25-30 minutes
- Total: 35-40 minutes

Servings:

- Number of servings: 2

Nutrition Information (per serving):

- Calories: approximately 350 kcal
- Protein: 30 g
- Fat: 25 g
- Carbohydrates: 0 g
- Fiber: 0 g
- Sugar: 0 g

STEAMED TURKEY WITH RICE

Ingredients:

- 2 turkey breast fillets
- Salt and pepper to taste
- 1 cup rice (white or brown)
- 2 cups chicken broth or water
- 1 tablespoon olive oil or butter
- 1 onion, finely chopped
- 2 cloves garlic, minced
- 1 teaspoon dried thyme
- 1 teaspoon dried sage
- 1/2 teaspoon paprika
- 1/2 teaspoon ground cumin
- Fresh parsley or cilantro for garnish (optional)
- Lemon wedges for serving (optional)

Directions:

1. Prepare the Rice:

- Run cold water over the rice until the water runs clear.
- In a saucepan, preheat the butter or olive oil over medium heat.
- Add chopped onion and minced garlic. Sauté for 2-3 minutes until softened and fragrant.
- Add dried thyme, dried sage, paprika, and ground cumin. Stir for another minute.

- Place the rice in the pot and toss to evenly distribute the onion and spice mixture over the rice.
- Include chicken broth or water. Bring to a boil, then reduce heat to a simmer, cover, and cook until the rice is soft and the liquid is absorbed, 15 to 20 minutes, or as per the instructions on the box. Take it off the heat and leave it covered for five minutes.

2. Prepare the Turkey:

- Season turkey breast fillets with salt and pepper on both sides.
- Prepare a steamer basket or a steamer insert in a large pot. Make sure the water in the pot is not too high to reach the steamer basket's bottom. Heat the water until it boils.

3. Steam Turkey:

- Place turkey breast fillets in the steamer basket or insert, ensuring they are not overcrowded.
- Cover the big pot with a lid and steam the turkey for 10-15 minutes until the turkey is cooked through.

4. Serve:

- Divide the rice with a fork among serving plates.
- Slice the steamed turkey breast fillets and arrange them on the rice.
- If preferred, garnish with fresh cilantro or parsley.
- Serve hot, optionally, with lemon wedges for squeezing over the turkey.

Prep Time:

- Preparation: 10 minutes
- Cooking (for rice and turkey): 30 minutes
- Total: 40 minutes

Servings:

- Number of servings: 2

Nutrition Information (per serving):

- Calories: approximately 400 kcal
- Protein: 30 g
- Fat: 10 g
- Carbohydrates: 45 g
- Fiber: 2 g
- Sugar: 2 g

VEGETABLE RAGOUT WITH BAKED TURKEY

Ingredients:

- 2 turkey breast fillets
- Salt and pepper to taste
- 2 tablespoons olive oil
- 1 onion, finely chopped
- 2 carrots, diced
- 2 celery stalks, diced
- 1 red bell pepper, diced
- 1 yellow bell pepper, diced
- 2 cloves garlic, minced
- 1 teaspoon dried thyme
- 1 teaspoon dried rosemary
- 1 teaspoon paprika
- 1/2 teaspoon ground cumin
- 1 can (14 oz) diced tomatoes
- 1 cup chicken broth
- 1 tablespoon tomato paste
- Salt and pepper to taste
- Fresh parsley or cilantro for garnish (optional)

Directions:

1. Prepare the Turkey:

- Preheat your oven to 375°F (190°C).
- Season turkey breast fillets with salt and pepper on both sides.
- In an oven-safe skillet, preheat 1 tablespoon of olive oil over medium-high heat.
- Sear the turkey breast fillets for 2-3 minutes per side until golden brown. Remove from the skillet and set aside.

2. Make the Vegetable Ragout:

- Add the last tablespoon of olive oil to the same skillet.
- Add chopped onion, carrots, celery, and bell peppers.
- Sauté for 5-7 minutes or until the vegetables start to soften.

3. Add Seasonings and Tomatoes:

- Add minced garlic, dried thyme, rosemary, paprika, and ground cumin to the skillet. Stir for 1 minute until fragrant.
- Stir in diced tomatoes (with their juices), chicken broth, and tomato paste.
- Season with salt and pepper to taste.
- Simmer the mixture for 9 to 13 minutes, stirring now and again, until the veggies are soft and the sauce has slightly thickened.

4. Bake the Turkey and Finish:

- Nestle the seared turkey breast fillets into the vegetable ragout in the skillet.
- Transfer the skillet to the preheated oven.
- Bake for 16-21 minutes until the turkey is cooked through.

5. Serve:

- Remove the skillet from the oven and let it rest for a few minutes.
- If preferred, garnish with fresh cilantro or parsley.
- Slice the turkey breast fillets and serve hot with the vegetable ragout.

Prep Time:

- Preparation: 15 minutes
- Cooking: 40 minutes
- Total: 55 minutes

Servings:

- Number of servings: 4

Nutrition Information (per serving):

- Calories: approximately 300 kcal
- Protein: 30 g
- Fat: 10 g
- Carbohydrates: 20 g
- Fiber: 5 g
- Sugar: 8 g

BAKED TROUT RECIPE

Ingredients:

- 2 whole trout, cleaned and gutted
- Salt and pepper to taste
- 2 tablespoons olive oil
- 2 cloves garlic, minced
- 1 lemon, thinly sliced
- Fresh herbs for garnishing, such as dill, thyme, or parsley
- Lemon wedges for serving

Directions:

1. Preheat the Oven:

- Preheat your oven to 400°F (200°C).

2. Prepare the Trout:

- Use paper towels to gently dry the fish after rinsing it in cold water.
- Liberally season the fish on the exterior and interior with salt and pepper.

3. Stuff and Season:

- Place minced garlic and lemon slices inside the cavity of each trout.
- Brush the outside of the trout with olive oil and season with additional sea salt and pepper if desired.

4. Bake the Trout:

- Arrange the yummy fish on a baking sheet covered with aluminum foil or parchment paper.
- Bake for 15 to 20 minutes, or until the meat is opaque throughout and flakes readily with a fork.

5. Serve:

- Carefully transfer the baked trout to serving plates.
- Serve hot with lemon wedges on the side.

Prep Time:

- Preparation: 10 minutes
- Cooking: 15-20 minutes
- Total: 25-30 minutes

Servings:

- Number of servings: 2

Nutrition Information (per serving):

- Calories: approximately 300 kcal
- Protein: 30 g
- Fat: 18 g
- Carbohydrates: 2 g
- Fiber: 1 g
- Sugar: 0 g

SEABASS WITH POTATOES, CAPERS, AND TOMATOES

Ingredients:

- 2 seabass fillets
- Salt and pepper to taste
- 2 tablespoons olive oil
- 1 lb (450g) baby potatoes, halved
- 2 cloves garlic, minced
- 1 pint cherry tomatoes, halved
- 2 tablespoons capers, drained
- 1 tablespoon fresh lemon juice
- Zest of 1 lemon
- Fresh parsley, chopped, for garnish
- Lemon wedges for serving

Directions:

1. Preheat the Oven:

- Preheat your oven to 400°F (200°C).

2. Prepare the Seabass:

- Season seabass fillets with salt and pepper on both sides.

3. Cook the Potatoes:

- Heat 1 tablespoon of olive oil in an oven-safe skillet over medium-high heat.

- When the potatoes are just browned, add the halved baby potatoes to the pan and simmer, turning periodically, for five to seven minutes.

4. Add Garlic and Tomatoes:

- Add minced garlic to the skillet with potatoes and cook for 1 minute until fragrant.
- Stir in cherry tomatoes and capers. Sauté until tomatoes begin to soften, another 2 to 3 minutes.

5. Prepare the Seabass:

- To make room for the seabass fillets, push the potato mixture to the sides of the skillet.
- Place seabass fillets in the center of the skillet, skin-side down if they have skin.

6. Bake:

- Drizzle the seabass fillets with the remaining tablespoon of olive oil.
- Place the pan in the oven that has been prepared, and bake for 12 to 15 minutes, or until the seabass is cooked through and flakes readily when tested with a fork.

7. Finish and Serve:

- Remove the skillet from the oven.
- Drizzle fresh lemon juice over the seabass and potato mixture.
- Sprinkle with lemon zest and chopped parsley.
- Present warm, with wedges of lemon on the side.

Prep Time:

- Preparation: 10 minutes
- Cooking: 25 minutes
- Total: 35 minutes

Servings:

- Number of servings: 2

Nutrition Information (per serving):

- Calories: approximately 400 kcal
- Protein: 30 g
- Fat: 15 g
- Carbohydrates: 35 g
- Fiber: 5 g
- Sugar: 5 g

ROSEMARY SHRIMP

Ingredients:

- 1 lb (450g) large shrimp, peeled and deveined
- 2 tablespoons olive oil
- 4 cloves garlic, minced
- 2-3 sprigs fresh rosemary
- Salt and pepper to taste
- Lemon wedges for serving
- Fresh parsley, chopped, for garnish (optional)

Directions:

1. Prepare the Shrimp:
- Use paper towels to pat the shrimp dry, then season with salt and pepper.

2. Cook the Shrimp:
- In a big skillet, warm up the olive oil over medium-high heat.
- Add minced garlic and fresh rosemary sprigs to the skillet. Cook for about 1 minute until fragrant.

3. Add the Shrimp:
- Arrange the seasoned shrimp in a single layer in the skillet. Cook for 2-3 minutes per side or until shrimp are pink and cooked through. Remove rosemary sprigs after cooking.

4. Serve:
- Spoon the cooked shrimp onto a platter for serving.

- If preferred, garnish with freshly chopped parsley.
- Present warm, with wedges of lemon on the side.

Prep Time:

- Preparation: 10 minutes
- Cooking: 10 minutes
- Total: 20 minutes

Servings:

- Number of servings: 4

Nutrition Information (per serving):

- Calories: approximately 200 kcal
- Protein: 25 g
- Fat: 9 g
- Carbohydrates: 1 g
- Fiber: 0 g
- Sugar: 0 g

MEDITERRANEAN ROASTED VEGETABLE LASAGNA

Ingredients:

- 1 eggplant, sliced into 1/4-inch rounds
- 2 zucchinis, sliced lengthwise into 1/4-inch strips
- One red bell pepper, seeded and sliced into strips
- One yellow bell pepper, seeded and sliced into strips
- 1 onion, thinly sliced
- 3 cloves garlic, minced
- 2 tablespoons olive oil
- Salt and pepper to taste
- 1 teaspoon dried oregano
- 1 teaspoon dried basil
- 1 can (15 oz) crushed tomatoes
- 1/2 cup tomato sauce
- Nine lasagna noodles prepared per the directions on the box
- 1 cup ricotta cheese
- 1 cup shredded mozzarella cheese
- 1/2 cup grated Parmesan cheese
- Fresh basil leaves for garnish

Directions:

1. Roast the Vegetables:

- Preheat the oven to 400°F (200°C).
- Place eggplant slices, zucchini strips, red and yellow bell pepper strips, and sliced onion on a large baking sheet.
- Drizzle with olive oil and season with salt, pepper, dried basil, dried oregano, and chopped garlic. For an even coat, toss.
- Roast in the oven for 20-25 minutes or until vegetables are tender and slightly caramelized. Remove from oven and set aside.

2. Prepare the Sauce:

- In a saucepan, combine crushed tomatoes and tomato sauce. Bring to a simmer over medium heat. Cook for 5-7 minutes, stirring occasionally—season with salt and pepper to taste. Remove from heat and set aside.

3. Assemble the Lasagna:

- Reduce oven temperature to 375°F (190°C).
- Lightly coat the bottom of a 9 by 13-inch baking dish with tomato sauce.
- Arrange 3 cooked lasagna noodles over the sauce.
- Spread half of the roasted vegetables evenly over the noodles.
- Dollop half of the ricotta cheese over the vegetables.
- Top with one-third of the Parmesan and mozzarella cheese.
- Repeat with remaining roasted veggies, 1/3 of mozzarella and Parmesan cheese, remaining ricotta cheese, and three more lasagna noodles.
- Place the last three lasagna noodles on top, then drizzle the leftover tomato sauce over them.
- Sprinkle with the remaining mozzarella and Parmesan cheese.

4. Bake the Lasagna:

- Cover the baking dish with foil and bake in the oven for 30 minutes.
- Take off the foil and bake the cheese for ten to fifteen minutes or until it is bubbling and browned.

5. Serve:

- Remove from the oven and let the lasagna rest for 10 minutes before slicing.
- Garnish with fresh basil leaves before serving.

Prep Time:

- Preparation: 30 minutes

- Cooking: 1 hour
- Total: 1 hour 30 minutes

Servings:

- Number of servings: 8

Nutrition Information (per serving):

- Calories: approximately 350 kcal
- Protein: 18 g
- Fat: 15 g
- Carbohydrates: 35 g
- Fiber: 5 g
- Sugar: 8 g

COD WITH CELERY CREAM

Ingredients:

- 4 cod fillets (about 6 oz each)
- Salt and pepper to taste
- 2 tablespoons olive oil
- 1 tablespoon butter
- 1 onion, finely chopped
- 2 cloves garlic, minced
- 4 cups celery root (celeriac), peeled and diced
- 1 cup chicken or vegetable broth
- 1/2 cup heavy cream
- 1/4 cup chopped fresh parsley
- Lemon wedges for serving

Directions:

1. Prepare the Cod:

- Pat the cod fillets dry with paper towels—season both sides with salt and pepper.

2. Cook the Cod:

- In a big skillet, warm up the olive oil over medium-high heat.
- Add cod fillets to the skillet and cook for about 4-5 minutes per side, or until fish flakes easily with a fork and is cooked through. Remove from skillet and set aside.

3. Make the Celery Cream Sauce:

- Melt butter over medium heat in the same pan.
- Add chopped onion and minced garlic. Sauté for 3-4 minutes until the onion is softened and translucent.

4. Cook the Celery Root:

- Add diced celery root (celeriac) to the skillet. Cook, stirring periodically, until celery root is tender, 5 to 7 minutes.

5. Simmer with Broth:

- Pour in chicken or vegetable broth. After bringing to a boil, turn down the heat. Cover and simmer for 15-20 minutes, or until celery root is tender and most liquid evaporates.

6. Blend and Add Cream:

- Pour the cooked combination of celery roots into a food processor or blender. Process till smooth.
- Place the combined mixture back in the skillet and turn the heat down.
- Stir in freshly chopped parsley and heavy cream. Add salt and pepper to taste. Cook, stirring periodically, for 2 to 3 minutes or until heated through and slightly thickened.

7. Serve:

- Spoon the celery cream sauce over the cooked cod fillets.
- Serve hot.

Prep Time:

- Preparation: 15 minutes
- Cooking: 30 minutes
- Total: 45 minutes

Servings:

- Number of servings: 4

Nutrition Information (per serving):

- Calories: approximately 350 kcal
- Protein: 30 g
- Fat: 18 g
- Carbohydrates: 15 g
- Fiber: 3 g
- Sugar: 4 g

BAKED DORADO WITH TOMATOES AND CAPERS

Ingredients:

- 4 Dorado fillets (about 6 oz each), skin-on
- Salt and pepper to taste
- 2 tablespoons olive oil
- 2 cloves garlic, minced
- 1 pint cherry tomatoes, halved
- 2 tablespoons capers, drained
- 1 lemon, thinly sliced
- 1/4 cup white wine (optional)
- Fresh parsley, chopped, for garnish

Directions:

1. Preheat the Oven:

- Preheat your oven to 400°F (200°C).

2. Prepare the Dorado Fillets:

- Pat the Dorado fillets dry with paper towels—season both sides with salt and pepper.

3. Sauté the Tomatoes and Capers:

- Heat the olive oil in a pan that is oven-safe over medium-high heat.
- Add the minced garlic and cook it until fragrant, about 1 minute.

- Add halved cherry tomatoes and capers to the skillet. Cook for 3-4 minutes, stirring occasionally, until tomatoes soften.

4. Add the Dorado Fillets:

- Push the tomatoes and capers to the sides of the skillet to make space for the dorado fillets.
- Place the fillets skin-side down in the skillet, nestled among the tomatoes and capers.

5. Add Lemon and Wine (if using):

- Arrange lemon slices over the dorado fillets.
- Pour white wine around the fillets in the skillet (if using).

6. Bake the Dorado:

- Transfer the skillet to the preheated oven.
- Bake the dorado fillets for 12 to 15 minutes or until they are cooked through and flake readily with a fork.

7. Serve:

- Remove from the oven and let rest for a few minutes.
- Garnish with chopped fresh parsley.
- Serve hot, spooning the tomato-caper mixture and pan juices over the dorado fillets.

Prep Time:

- Preparation: 10 minutes
- Cooking: 15 minutes
- Total: 25 minutes

Servings:

- Number of servings: 4

Nutrition Information (per serving):

- Calories: approximately 250 kcal
- Protein: 30 g
- Fat: 12 g
- Carbohydrates: 6 g
- Fiber: 2 g
- Sugar: 3 g

DORADO WITH LEMON

Ingredients:

- 4 Dorado fillets (about 6 oz each), skin-on
- Salt and pepper to taste
- 2 tablespoons olive oil
- 2 lemons, thinly sliced
- Fresh parsley, chopped, for garnish
- Lemon wedges for serving

Directions:

1. Preheat the Oven:

- Preheat your oven to 400°F (200°C).

2. Prepare the Dorado Fillets:

- Pat the Dorado fillets dry with paper towels. Season both sides generously with salt and pepper.

3. Arrange in Baking Dish:

- Drizzle olive oil over the bottom of a baking dish.
- Place the dorado fillets skin-side down in the baking dish, spaced evenly apart.

4. Add Lemon Slices:

- Arrange lemon slices over each dorado fillet.

5. Bake the Dorado:

- After preheating the oven, move the baking dish inside.
- Bake for 15 to 20 minutes or until the dorado fillets are tender and flake readily with a fork.

6. Serve:

- Remove from the oven and let rest for a few minutes.
- Garnish with chopped fresh parsley.
- Serve hot. You can add lemon for both sides.

Prep Time:

- Preparation: 5 minutes
- Cooking: 15-20 minutes
- Total: 20-25 minutes

Servings:

- Number of servings: 4

Nutrition Information (per serving):

- Calories: approximately 250 kcal
- Protein: 30 g
- Fat: 12 g
- Carbohydrates: 5 g
- Fiber: 2 g
- Sugar: 1 g

TUNA AND POTATO CASSEROLE

Ingredients:

- 4 large potatoes, peeled and thinly sliced
- 2 cans (5 oz each) tuna, drained and flaked
- 1 onion, finely chopped
- 1 red bell pepper, diced
- 1 cup frozen peas
- 1 cup grated cheddar cheese
- 1/2 cup heavy cream
- 1/2 cup milk
- 2 tablespoons olive oil
- Salt and pepper to taste
- Fresh parsley, chopped, for garnish

Directions:

1. Preheat the Oven:

- Preheat your oven to 375°F (190°C).

2. Prepare Potatoes:

- Place the sliced potatoes in a large pot of salted boiling water. Cook for 5-7 minutes, until slightly tender. Drain and set aside.

3. Sauté Onion and Bell Pepper:

- Heat olive oil in a large skillet over medium heat.
- Add chopped onion and diced red bell pepper. Sauté for 5-7 minutes until softened.

4. Assemble the Casserole:

- Arrange half of the cooked potatoes in a baking dish that has been buttered.
- Spread half of the flaked tuna over the potatoes.
- Sprinkle half of the sautéed onion and bell pepper mixture on top.
- Sprinkle half the frozen peas and half the grated cheddar cheese over the vegetables.

5. Repeat Layers:

- Repeat the layers with the remaining potatoes, tuna, onion, bell pepper mixture, peas, and cheddar cheese.

6. Prepare the Cream Mixture:

- Whisk together heavy cream, milk, salt, and pepper in a bowl.
- Pour the cream mixture evenly over the casserole.

7. Bake the Casserole:

- Bake the baking dish for 29-30 minutes in the oven, covered with foil.
- Take off the foil and bake for 15 to 20 minutes or until the top is bubbling and golden brown.

8. Serve:

- Remove from the oven. Let rest for 5 minutes.
- Garnish with chopped fresh parsley before serving.

Prep Time:

- Preparation: 20 minutes
- Cooking: 45-50 minutes
- Total: 1 hour 5 minutes

Servings:

- Number of servings: 6

Nutrition Information (per serving):

- Calories: approximately 400 kcal
- Protein: 25 g
- Fat: 20 g
- Carbohydrates: 30 g
- Fiber: 4 g
- Sugar: 5 g

LAMB WITH BEANS AND GREEN BEANS

Ingredients:

- 1 lb (450g) lamb shoulder or leg, diced
- Salt and pepper to taste
- 2 tablespoons olive oil
- 1 onion, finely chopped
- 2 cloves garlic, minced
- 1 carrot, diced
- 1 celery stalk, diced
- One cup of green beans, trimmed and cut into bite-sized pieces
- One cup of canned white beans drained and rinsed
- One cup of chicken or vegetable broth
- 1 tablespoon tomato paste
- 1 teaspoon dried thyme
- 1 bay leaf
- Fresh parsley, chopped, for garnish

Directions:

1. Season and Sear the Lamb:

- Season diced lamb with salt and pepper.
- Heat Italian olive oil in a large pot or Dutch oven over medium-high heat.

- Add lamb and brown on all sides, about 5-7 minutes. Take out the lamb from the pot and set aside.

2. Sauté Vegetables:

- Add chopped onion, minced garlic, diced carrot, and diced celery in the same pot.
- Sauté for 5 minutes, until vegetables are softened.

3. Combine Ingredients:

- Return the browned lamb to the pot.
- Include the bay leaf, dried thyme, tomato paste, white beans, chicken or vegetable broth, and green beans.5
- Stir to combine well.

4. Simmer:

- After bringing the mixture to a boil, turn down the heat.
- Simmer the lamb, covered, stirring often, for 1.5 to 2 hours or until the flavors have blended and the meat is tender.

5. Serve:

- Remove bay leaf before serving.
- Garnish with chopped fresh parsley.
- Serve hot, optionally with crusty bread or over rice.

Prep Time:

- Preparation: 15 minutes
- Cooking: 1.5 - 2 hours
- Total: 1 hour 45 minutes - 2 hours 15 minutes

Servings:

- Number of servings: 4

Nutrition Information (per serving):

- Calories: approximately 400 kcal
- Protein: 30 g
- Fat: 20 g
- Carbohydrates: 20 g
- Fiber: 6 g
- Sugar: 4 g

MEDITERRANEAN-STYLE MUSSELS

Ingredients:

- 2 lbs (about 1 kg) fresh mussels, cleaned and debearded
- 2 tablespoons olive oil
- 4 cloves garlic, minced
- 1 onion, finely chopped
- 1 red bell pepper, diced
- 1 yellow bell pepper, diced
- 1 can (14 oz or 400g) diced tomatoes
- 1/2 cup dry white wine
- 1/4 cup chopped fresh parsley
- 1 teaspoon dried oregano
- Salt and pepper to taste
- Crushed red pepper flakes (optional)
- Crusty bread for serving

Directions:

1. Prepare the Mussels:

- Scrub the mussels under cold water to remove any dirt or debris.
- Pull out the beards (strings) if they are still attached. Discard any mussels that are open and do not close when tapped.

2. Sauté Aromatics:

- Heat olive oil in a large pot or Dutch oven over medium heat.

- Add minced garlic and chopped onion. Sauté for 2-3 minutes until fragrant and onions are translucent.

3. *Add Bell Peppers and Tomatoes:*

- Add diced yellow and red bell peppers and stir. Cook until peppers start to soften, about 3 to 4 minutes more.
- Fill the saucepan with diced tomatoes and their liquids. Mix well to blend.

4. *Simmer with Wine and Herbs:*

- Add dried oregano and pour in dry white wine.
- Season with crushed red pepper flakes, salt, and pepper (if using).
- To enable the flavors to mingle, bring the mixture to a simmer and cook for five to seven minutes.

5. *Cook the Mussels:*

- Add cleaned mussels to the pot.
- Cover with a lid and cook over medium heat for 5-7 minutes, shaking the pot occasionally until the mussels have opened. Discard any mussels that do not open.

6. *Finish and Serve:*

- Remove the pot from heat.
- Stir in chopped fresh parsley.
- Serve hot, spooning mussels and broth into bowls.
- Accompany with toasted bread for dipping into the aromatic broth.

Prep Time:

- Preparation: 20 minutes
- Cooking: 20 minutes
- Total: 40 minutes

Servings:

- Number of servings: 4

Nutrition Information (per serving):

- Calories: approximately 250 kcal
- Protein: 25 g
- Fat: 8 g
- Carbohydrates: 15 g
- Fiber: 3 g
- Sugar: 5 g

PAN-FRIED CALAMARI WITH GARLIC AND OLIVES

Ingredients:

- 1 lb (450g) calamari tubes, cleaned and sliced into rings
- 1/2 cup all-purpose flour
- Salt and pepper to taste
- 2 tablespoons olive oil
- 4 cloves garlic, minced
- 1/2 cup pitted green olives, sliced
- 2 tablespoons fresh parsley, chopped
- Lemon wedges for serving

Directions:

1. Prepare the Calamari:

- Rinse the calamari under cold water and pat dry with paper towels.
- Slice the calamari tubes into rings and set aside.

2. Coat the Calamari:

- Put the all-purpose flour, salt, and pepper to taste in a small dish.
- Dredge the calamari rings in the seasoned flour, shaking off any excess.

3. Heat Olive Oil:

- Heat olive oil in a large skillet over medium-high heat.

4. Cook the Calamari:

- Add the minced garlic to the skillet and sauté it for about a minute, or until it becomes aromatic, once the oil is heated.
- Add the floured calamari rings to the skillet in a single layer (work in batches if necessary to avoid overcrowding).
- Cook the calamari for 2-3 minutes per side until golden brown and crispy.

5. Add Olives:

- Add sliced green olives to the skillet at the last minute of cooking, tossing gently to combine them with the calamari.

6. Serve:

- Remove the skillet from heat.
- Sprinkle chopped fresh parsley over the calamari and olives.
- Serve hot, with lemon wedges on the side to squeeze over the calamari.

Prep Time:

- Preparation: 15 minutes
- Cooking: 10 minutes
- Total: 25 minutes

Servings:

- Number of servings: 4

Nutrition Information (per serving):

- Calories: approximately 300 kcal
- Protein: 25 g
- Fat: 12 g
- Carbohydrates: 20 g
- Fiber: 2 g
- Sugar: 1 g

BEEF TENDERLOIN WITH ROSEMARY

Ingredients:

- 1 beef tenderloin (about 2 lbs or 900g), trimmed
- 2 tablespoons olive oil
- 4 cloves garlic, minced
- 2 tablespoons fresh rosemary, chopped
- Salt and pepper to taste

Directions:

1. Preheat the Oven:

- Preheat your oven to 400°F (200°C).

2. Prepare the Beef Tenderloin:

- Use paper towels to pat dry the beef tenderloin.
- Liberally season on all sides with salt and pepper.

3. Sear the Beef:

- In a large ovenproof skillet, heat the oil made from olives over medium-high heat.
- Add the chopped rosemary and minced garlic to the pan and stir until fragrant, about 1 minute.
- Place the seasoned beef tenderloin in the skillet and sear for 2-3 minutes on each side until nicely browned.

4. Roast the Tenderloin:

- Place the pan with the seared beef tenderloin in the oven that has been preheated.

- Roast for 15 to 20 minutes, or until the desired doneness, or 135°F (57°C), is read with a meat thermometer put into the thickest portion of the flesh.

5. Rest and Serve:

- Take the pan out of the oven and set the tenderloin aside on a chopping board.
- Before slicing, tent loosely with foil and give it ten minutes to rest.

6. Slice and Serve:

- Slice the beef tenderloin against the grain into thick slices.
- Serve warm, garnished with additional fresh rosemary if desired.

Prep Time:

- Preparation: 10 minutes
- Cooking: 25 minutes
- Total: 35 minutes

Servings:

- Number of servings: 4-6

Nutrition Information (per serving):

- Calories: approximately 350 kcal
- Protein: 40 g
- Fat: 20 g
- Carbohydrates: 1 g
- Fiber: 0 g
- Sugar: 0 g

PITA BREAD WITH BEAN HUMMUS

Ingredients:

- 1 can (15 oz or 400g) chickpeas, drained and rinsed
- 1/4 cup tahini (sesame seed paste)
- 2 cloves garlic, minced
- 2 tablespoons olive oil
- 2 tablespoons lemon juice
- 1/2 teaspoon ground cumin
- Salt to taste
- 4 whole wheat pita bread rounds
- a quarter cup of fresh parsley chopped (for garnish only)
- 1 tablespoon olive oil (for drizzling, optional)

Directions:

1. Prepare the Bean Hummus:

- Combine chickpeas, tahini, minced garlic, olive oil, lemon juice, ground cumin, and salt in a food processor.
- Process until smooth and creamy, adding a little water to achieve desired consistency. Adjust seasoning to taste.

2. Warm the Pita Bread:

- Preheat oven to 350°F (175°C).
- Arrange the rounds of pita bread on a baking sheet and bake for five to seven minutes or until cooked through.

3. Assemble the Pita with Hummus:
- Spread a generous amount of bean hummus on each warmed pita bread round.

4. Garnish and Serve:
- Sprinkle chopped fresh parsley over the hummus (if using).
- Drizzle with a bit of olive oil for extra flavor (optional).
- Serve immediately while the pita bread is warm.

Prep Time:
- Preparation: 10 minutes
- Cooking: 5-7 minutes
- Total: 15-17 minutes

Servings:
- Number of servings: 4

Nutrition Information (per serving, without optional ingredients):
- Calories: approximately 300 kcal
- Protein: 10 g
- Fat: 12 g
- Carbohydrates: 35 g
- Fiber: 8 g
- Sugar: 1 g

PAN-SEARED HALIBUT

Ingredients:

- 4 halibut fillets, about 6 oz (170g) each
- Salt and pepper to taste
- 2 tablespoons olive oil
- 2 tablespoons butter
- 2 cloves garlic, minced
- 1 tablespoon fresh lemon juice
- 2 tablespoons chopped fresh parsley

Directions:

1. Season the Halibut:

- Pat dry the halibut fillets with paper towels—season both sides with salt and pepper.

2. Heat the Pan:

- Heat the olive oil in a big pan over medium-high heat until it shimmers.

3. Cook the Halibut:

- Place the halibut fillets in the skillet, skin side down if skin-on, and cook for 4-5 minutes without moving them. This allows a golden crust to form.
- Using a spatula, carefully turn the fillets over and continue cooking for a further 3-4 minutes or until the salmon is opaque and flakes readily.

4. Add Butter and Garlic:

- Fill the skillet with minced garlic and butter. Fish should be cooked for approximately a minute while butter is spooned over it to baste.

5. Finish and Serve:

- Remove the skillet from heat. Drizzle the halibut fillets with freshly squeezed lemon juice and garnish with finely chopped fresh parsley.

6. Serve:

- Serve the pan-seared halibut immediately, garnished with additional parsley if desired.

Prep Time:

- Preparation: 10 minutes
- Cooking: 10 minutes
- Total: 20 minutes

Servings:

- Number of servings: 4

Nutrition Information (per serving):

- Calories: approximately 300 kcal
- Protein: 34 g
- Fat: 17 g
- Carbohydrates: 1 g
- Fiber: 0 g
- Sugar: 0 g

SEABASS WITH LEEKS

Ingredients:

- 4 seabass fillets, skin-on, about 6 oz (170g) each
- Salt and pepper to taste
- 2 tablespoons olive oil
- Thinly sliced leeks with white and light green sections
- 2 cloves garlic, minced
- 1/2 cup dry white wine
- 1/2 cup chicken or vegetable broth
- 2 tablespoons fresh lemon juice
- 2 tablespoons chopped fresh parsley
- Lemon wedges for serving

Directions:

1. Season the Seabass:

- Pat dry the seabass fillets with paper towels—season both sides with salt and pepper.

2. Sear the Seabass:

- Heat the olive oil in a big pan over medium-high heat. Seabass fillets should be placed upside down in the skillet and cooked for 4-5 minutes or until the skin is crispy and golden. When the fish is done and flakes readily with a fork, carefully flip the fillets over and continue cooking for an additional 3-4 minutes. After taking the seabass out of the pan, set it aside.

3. Cook the Leeks:

- In the same skillet, add sliced leeks and minced garlic. Sauté for 2-3 minutes until leeks are softened.

4. Deglaze the Pan:

- Add the white wine and broth (either chicken or veggie). Simmer while scraping off any browned bits from the skillet's bottom.

5. Finish the Sauce:

- Simmer for 3-4 minutes or until half of the liquid has evaporated. Stir in chopped parsley and freshly squeezed lemon juice.

6. Serve:

- Return the seabass fillets to the skillet, spooning the leek mixture over the top. Cook for another minute to warm the fish through.
- Serve the seabass with leeks immediately, garnished with lemon wedges.

Prep Time:

- Preparation: 10 minutes
- Cooking: 15 minutes
- Total: 25 minutes

Servings:

- Number of servings: 4

Nutrition Information (per serving):

- Calories: approximately 250 kcal
- Protein: 30 g
- Fat: 11 g
- Carbohydrates: 5 g
- Fiber: 1 g
- Sugar: 2 g

CHICKEN WITH MUSHROOMS IN CREAMY SAUCE

Ingredients:

- 4 boneless, skinless chicken breasts
- Salt and pepper to taste
- 2 tablespoons olive oil
- 2 tablespoons butter
- 8 oz (225g) mushrooms, sliced
- 2 cloves garlic, minced
- 1/2 cup chicken broth
- 1 cup heavy cream
- 1 teaspoon dried thyme (or 1 tablespoon fresh thyme leaves)
- 1/4 cup grated Parmesan cheese
- Fresh parsley, chopped (for garnish)
- Lemon wedges (optional for serving)

Directions:

Prepare the Chicken:

- Season both sides of the chicken breasts with salt and pepper.

Sear the Chicken:

- In a large skillet, heat olive oil over medium-high heat. Add chicken breasts and cook for 5-6 minutes per side or until golden brown and cooked through. Remove chicken from skillet and set aside.

Cook the Mushrooms:

- In the same skillet, melt butter. Add sliced mushrooms and minced garlic. Sauté for 4-5 minutes until mushrooms are tender and browned.

Make the Sauce:

- Add the chicken broth and boil, scraping off any brown pieces from the skillet's bottom.
- Stir in the dried thyme and heavy cream. Cook, stirring periodically, for 3-4 minutes or until the sauce thickens slightly.

Combine and Finish:

- Place the chicken breasts back in the skillet, tucking them in between the mushrooms and sauce. To fully cook the chicken, simmer it for a further two to three minutes.
- Sprinkle-grated Parmesan cheese over the chicken and sauce. Stir gently to combine and allow the cheese to melt.

Serve:

- Garnish with chopped fresh parsley.
- Serve with lemon wedges, and enjoy!

Prep Time:

- Preparation: 10 minutes
- Cooking: 20 minutes
- Total: 30 minutes

Servings:

- Number of servings: 4

Nutrition Information (per serving):

- Calories: approximately 450 kcal
- Protein: 30 g
- Fat: 33 g
- Carbohydrates: 7 g
- Fiber: 1 g
- Sugar: 2 g

GRILLED TUNA WITH HERB AIOLI

Ingredients:

- 4 tuna steaks, about 6 oz (170g) each
- Salt and pepper to taste
- 2 tablespoons olive oil

For the Herb Aioli:

- 1/2 cup mayonnaise
- 1 clove garlic, minced
- 1 tablespoon fresh lemon juice
- 1 tablespoon chopped fresh parsley
- 1 tablespoon chopped fresh basil
- Salt and pepper to taste

Directions:

1. Prepare the Herb Aioli:

- In a small bowl, combine mayonnaise, minced garlic, fresh lemon juice, chopped parsley, and chopped basil—season with salt and pepper to taste. Mix well. Cover and refrigerate until ready to use.

2. Grill the Tuna:

- Turn the heat up to medium-high on the grill or grill pan.
- The tuna steaks should be pat-dried using paper towels. Use salt and pepper to season both sides.
- Brush olive oil over the tuna steaks to lightly coat.

- Grill the tuna steaks for 3-4 minutes per side or until grill marks form and the tuna is cooked to your desired doneness. The internal temperature should reach about 125°F (52°C) for medium-rare.

3. Serve:

- Remove grilled tuna steaks from the grill and rest for a few minutes.
- Serve hot, topped with a dollop of herb aioli on each steak.

Prep Time:

- Preparation: 10 minutes
- Cooking: 8 minutes
- Total: 18 minutes

Servings:

- Number of servings: 4

Nutrition Information (per serving):

- Calories: approximately 350 kcal
- Protein: 30 g
- Fat: 25 g
- Carbohydrates: 2 g
- Fiber: 0 g
- Sugar: 1 g

SALMON AND AVOCADO TARTARE

Ingredients:

- 12 oz (340g) fresh salmon fillet, skinless and boneless
- 1 ripe avocado, diced
- 1 tablespoon red onion, finely chopped
- 1 tablespoon capers, drained and chopped
- 1 tablespoon fresh dill, chopped
- 1 tablespoon fresh parsley, chopped
- Zest and juice of 1 lemon
- 2 tablespoons extra virgin olive oil
- Salt and pepper to taste
- Optional: microgreens or lettuce leaves for serving

Directions:

1. Prepare the Salmon:

- Cut the salmon fillet into small cubes, about 1/4 inch (0.6 cm) in size. Place the salmon cubes in a mixing bowl.

2. Mix the Ingredients:

- Add diced avocado, chopped red onion, capers, fresh dill, and fresh parsley to the bowl with the salmon.

3. Add Lemon Zest and Juice:

- Finely grate one lemon's zest straight into the basin.
- Squeeze the juice of the lemon over the salmon mixture.

4. Season and Dress:

- Drizzle extra virgin olive oil over the salmon mixture—season with salt and pepper to taste.

5. Combine Gently:

- Gently mix all the ingredients until well-mixed. Be careful not to mash the avocado too much.

6. Chill and Serve:

- To let the flavors melt together, cover the bowl with plastic wrap and chill for 15 to 20 minutes.

Serve:

- When ready to serve, spoon the salmon and avocado tartare onto plates or into bowls. Optionally, garnish with microgreens or serve on a bed of lettuce leaves.

Prep Time:

- Preparation: 15 minutes
- Chilling: 20 minutes
- Total: 35 minutes

Servings:

- Number of servings: 4

Nutrition Information (per serving):

- Calories: approximately 250 kcal
- Protein: 20 g
- Fat: 17 g
- Carbohydrates: 6 g
- Fiber: 4 g
- Sugar: 1 g

LAMB WITH PLUMS

Ingredients:
- 1 lb (450g) lamb shoulder or leg, cut into cubes
- Salt and pepper to taste
- 2 tablespoons olive oil
- 1 onion, finely chopped
- 2 cloves garlic, minced
- 1 teaspoon ground cumin
- 1 teaspoon ground coriander
- 1/2 teaspoon ground cinnamon
- 1/2 teaspoon ground ginger
- 1/4 teaspoon cayenne pepper (optional for heat)
- 1 cup chicken or lamb broth
- 1/2 cup dried plums (prunes), pitted
- 1 tablespoon honey or brown sugar
- Zest and juice of 1 lemon
- Fresh parsley or cilantro, chopped (for garnish)
- Cooked couscous or rice (for serving)

Directions:

1. Prepare the Lamb:
- Season the lamb cubes with salt and pepper.

2. Sear the Lamb:

- In a big skillet or Dutch oven, heat the olive oil over medium-high heat. Lamb cubes should be added in batches and browned all over. Lamb cubes should be removed and put aside.

3. Sauté the Aromatics:

- Add chopped onion and sauté in the same skillet for 3-4 minutes until softened. Add minced garlic and cook for another 1 minute until fragrant.

4. Add Spices:

- Stir in ground cumin, coriander, cinnamon, ginger, and cayenne pepper (if using). Cook for 1 minute to toast the spices.

5. Simmer with Broth:

- Return the lamb cubes to the skillet. Pour in chicken or lamb broth and bring to a simmer. Once the lamb is cooked, reduce heat to low, cover, and simmer gently for about 1 hour.

6. Add Plums and Sweeten:

- Add dried plums (prunes), honey or brown sugar, lemon zest, and juice to the skillet. Stir well to combine.

7. Finish and Serve:

- Simmer uncovered for another 10-15 minutes or until the sauce has thickened slightly.
- Adjust seasoning with salt and pepper if needed.
- Garnish with chopped fresh parsley or cilantro.
- Serve hot, overcooked couscous or rice.

Prep Time:

- Preparation: 15 minutes
- Cooking: 1 hour 30 minutes
- Total: 1 hour 45 minutes

Servings:

- Number of servings: 4

Nutrition Information (per serving, without couscous or rice):

- Calories: approximately 350 kcal
- Protein: 25 g
- Fat: 18 g

- Carbohydrates: 20 g
- Fiber: 3 g
- Sugar: 15 g

GRILLED SHRIMP WRAPPED IN PROSCIUTTO

Ingredients:

- 12 large shrimp, peeled and deveined
- 6 slices prosciutto, sliced in half lengthwise
- 1 tablespoon olive oil
- Salt and pepper to taste
- Wooden skewers, soaked in water for 30 minutes

Directions:

1. Prepare the Shrimp:

- Preheat the grill to medium-high heat.

2. Wrap Shrimp with Prosciutto:

- Season shrimp with salt and pepper. Wrap each shrimp with half a slice of prosciutto, securing it with a toothpick if needed.

3. Grill the Shrimp:

- To keep the grill grates from sticking, brush them with olive oil. Place the wrapped shrimp on the grill.

4. Grill Until Cooked:

- Grill the shrimp for two to three minutes on each side or until they are opaque and pink and the prosciutto is crispy.

5. Serve:

- Remove from the grill and serve hot.

Prep Time:

- Preparation: 10 minutes
- Cooking: 6 minutes
- Total: 16 minutes

Servings:

- Number of servings: 4 (3 shrimp per serving)

Nutrition Information (per serving):

- Calories: approximately 150 kcal
- Protein: 16 g
- Fat: 8 g
- Carbohydrates: 1 g
- Fiber: 0 g
- Sugar: 0 g

SEA TROUT WITH GRILLED ASPARAGUS AND LEMONS

Ingredients:

- 4 sea trout fillets, skin-on (about 6 oz/170g each)
- Salt and pepper to taste
- 1 bunch asparagus, trimmed
- 2 lemons, halved
- 2 tablespoons olive oil
- 2 cloves garlic, minced
- 1 tablespoon fresh thyme leaves
- Lemon wedges for serving
- Fresh parsley, chopped (for garnish)

Directions:

1. Prepare the Grill:

- Preheat a grill to medium-high heat.

2. Season the Sea Trout:

- Pat dry the sea trout fillets with paper towels—season both sides with salt and pepper.

3. Grill the Sea Trout:

- Rub the sea trout fillets with olive oil. Place them skin-side down on the preheated grill. Grill for 3-4 minutes on each side until the fish is cooked and flakes easily with a fork. Remove from heat and set aside.

4. Grill the Asparagus and Lemons:

- Toss the trimmed asparagus spears with olive oil, minced garlic, and fresh thyme leaves—season with salt and pepper to taste.
- Place the asparagus spears and lemon halves cut side down on the grill. Grill for 2-3 minutes per side or until the asparagus is tender-crisp, charred in spots, and the lemons are caramelized.

5. Serve:

- Arrange the grilled sea trout fillets on a serving platter.
- Place the grilled asparagus and caramelized lemon halves alongside the sea trout.
- Garnish with chopped fresh parsley.
- Serve immediately with additional lemon wedges.

Prep Time:

- Preparation: 10 minutes
- Cooking: 10 minutes
- Total: 20 minutes

Servings:

- Number of servings: 4

Nutrition Information (per serving):

- Calories: approximately 300 kcal
- Protein: 30 g
- Fat: 16 g
- Carbohydrates: 10 g
- Fiber: 4 g
- Sugar: 3 g

Printed in Great Britain
by Amazon